Contents

© Flammarion 1981
First English edition 1981
Macdonald & Co. Publishers
Holywell House
Worship Street
London EC2A 2EN

ISBN 0 356 06756 4 X

Printed in Italy by
A. Mondadori, Verona

Endpaper: An aerial combat scene involving a Messerschmitt Bf 110, and several Heinkel 111s and Hurricanes.

The Battle of Britain

by ANN TILBURY

illustrated by MICHAEL TURNER

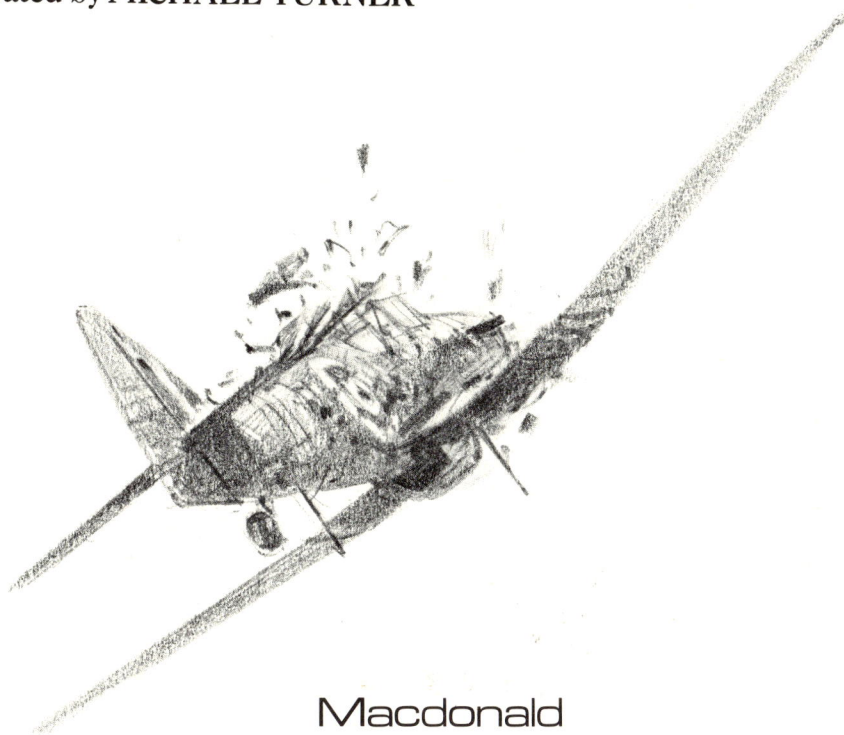

Macdonald

Dunkirk

Below: The deserted beach at Dunkirk after the British withdrawal. A Messerschmidt Bf 109 flies over the ingenious makeshift jetty and the wreck of a Spitfire.

The withdrawal of the British Expeditionary Force from Europe was authorized on 16 May 1940. Some of them had been over there since 12 September 1939. Outnumbered and outflanked as country after country fell to the Germans, they had retreated towards the coast at Dunkirk. They were pursued by tanks which, incredibly, halted some 20 kilometres away because the land was marshy and Hitler did not want his tanks bogged down. In any case, Göring, the Air Minister, wanted his prized Luftwaffe to wipe out the BEF.

Most of the Force managed the trek to Dunkirk, where they had to survive the best they could until Operation Dynamo (their evacuation) began. Ammunition and food were desperately short. The men sheltered where they could; in the ruins of the bombed town, in vehicles, or just in hollows scraped in the sand dunes. Exhausted, starving and, justifiably, frightened, they were further demoralized by being subjected to terrifying dive bombing by Stukas. Their bombs had cardboard whistles attached which made a horrifying scream as they hurtled down.

On May 26 the German army was once more ordered to attack, but the brief respite had allowed the Commander of the BEF, General Lord Gort, to organize some sort of defence of the area. All the remaining armaments were thrown into this defence. Nothing could be taken back to England and every hour that the Force could hold off the Germans counted. For at 18.57 on that same day the Admiralty had signalled the start of Operation Dynamo, and the strange assortment of vessels which had been assembled at ports along the Kent coast set out. There were trawlers, luxury yachts, ferries, racing boats, and even non-powered boats towed by tugs.

Dunkirk harbour had been destroyed, but there was still a wood and concrete mole (jetty). But the water was shallow, the tide went out for over a kilometre, there was a fresh south-westerly wind, the Channel was mined, and the Luftwaffe was still bombing and strafing the area. Army vehicles, and others which had been commandeered, were driven into the sea, roughly covered with planks, and used as a jetty to speed up the loading. Small boats ferried weary men to larger ships. Not-so-small ships crammed as many men on board as possible and headed for England. Coastal Command Hudsons flew protectively over the armada, but the Luftwaffe still made vast inroads.

Realizing that the net was emptying, Göring ordered an all-out attack on the beaches, which started on June 1. Where was the RAF? It was a bitter question asked by the besieged men on the beaches. Winston Churchill, British Prime Minister since May 10, was a Francophile. Despite the warnings of Air Chief Marshal Sir Hugh Dowding, Air Officer Commanding-in-Chief (AOC-in-C) Fighter Command, that 52 squadrons were the minimum necessary for the defence of Britain, he had sent squadron after squadron to France. Between May 10 and June 4 the RAF lost 432 fighters, mainly Hurricanes. Spitfires, Blenheims and Defiants were now being used as well, often backed up by out-dated Hectors and Lysanders.

Their tactics were to engage the enemy before he could attack the men on the beaches. When they were fighting over the coast, the men below could not see them because the cloud base was low. Flight-Lieutenant Brian Kingcombe described it as being like a pile of sandwiches, with clear air between the layers so that, from his Spitfire, he seldom saw the ground. The pilots were beyond British radar range, and so could not be directed to the enemy by ground control. They had to patrol the skies hoping to intercept the enemy. And in such cloud RAF and Luftwaffe pilots could pass within a few hundred metres and not see each other. These RAF fighters were from the forward bases at Biggin Hill, Manston, Lympne, Hawkinge and Kenley. They flew hundreds of sorties while the evacuation was taking place. Over 100 fighters were lost, but much more serious was the loss of some 80 experienced pilots. The loss of an experienced pilot was worse than the loss of 10 Spitfires. Dowding had barely 25 squadrons left. On June 1 the Luftwaffe broke through the RAF guard, sank three destroyers and various transports, and attacked the beaches more harshly than ever.

Then the incredible happened. Just as it seemed that Operation Dynamo was becoming unworkable due to the losses, the Luftwaffe was withdrawn to attack airfields around Paris. Had Hitler continued with his original plan, or Göring attacked for a few more days, the BEF would have been decimated. As it was, between May 26 and June 3 over 330,000 men, including many French, were saved by a makeshift armada of 887 boats. Both sides claimed Dunkirk as a victory, although as Churchill carefully pointed out, "wars are not won by evacuations".

Operation Sea Lion

The original plan to take the vital Channel ports had been a 1914-18 scheme starting with an attack through Belgium and northern France. Then *Generalleutnant* Fritz von Manstein, Chief of Staff of *Generaloberst* Gerd von Runstedt's Army Group A, suggested a seemingly outrageous plan: a thrust south through the Ardennes, which had been thought impassable to armoured vehicles, through Sedan and thus north to the Channel. Not only was there the element of surprise in this plan but, if successful, it would cut the Allied forces in two.

Germany invaded Poland on September 1, 1939, and then Denmark and Norway. On May 10, 1940 Holland was attacked by paratroops and Luxemburg and Belgium fell soon afterwards. The sound of the guns could be heard in England. On the French/Belgian border was the Maginot Line, "the greatest defensive fortification of all time. Before it, Hitler's vaunted war-machine hesitates". There was little hesitation as the "war-machine" went around, passing between the Maginot Line and the Belgian border. The direction of the thrust, and the speed (60 kilometres a day through France), was a surprise to the Allies. On May 21 the Germans reached the sea and could see England. The Luftwaffe, victorious in six countries, bombed the airfields around Paris and, on June 22, France sued for peace.

Below: Barges being prepared as landing craft, and troops assembling for the invasion of England.

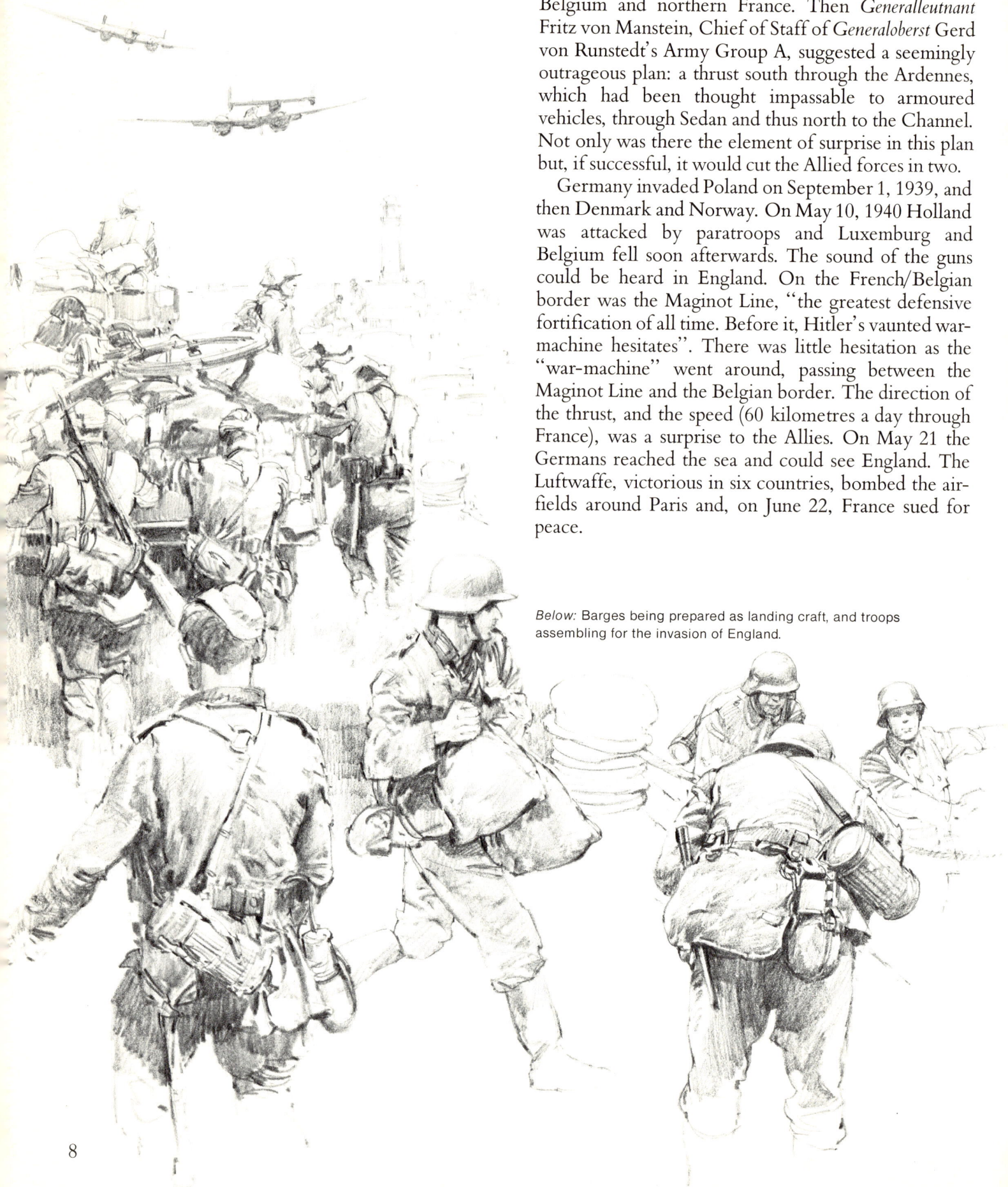

Hitler was so sure that Britain would now surrender that he disbanded 15 divisions. Had he attacked immediately after the debacle of Dunkirk, Britain might well have fallen. But Britain had been allowed time to get her breath back. She did not give in. On July 16 Hitler issued his Directive 16: "As England, despite her hopeless military situation, still shows no sign of willingness to come to terms, I have decided to prepare, and if necessary to carry out, a landing operation against her. The aim of this operation is to eliminate the English motherland as a base from which war against Germany can be continued and, if necessary, to occupy the country completely."

His deadline was mid-August, but this was later postponed. The German navy needed time to prepare. There were no landing craft available, and barges had to be obtained and adapted, and troops re-trained. The Luftwaffe had to make use of the time available. Royal Navy bases must be attacked so they could not disrupt the invasion (code-named Sea Lion). The Luftwaffe's task was to neutralize the RAF and take over the forward airfields such as Manston and Hawkinge.

The Luftwaffe now had bases from Norway to the Spanish coast. The fall of France had given them 50 bases in northern France and Holland. *Luftflotten* (air fleets) 2 and 3 were based in France and the Low Countries, with *Luftflotte* 5 based in Scandinavia. On the last day of June the Germans had landed in the Channel Islands, on Guernsey, and 24 hours later had occupied the islands; an occupation which was to last until May 1945.

With northern Europe in enemy hands there was a serious lack of military intelligence, and high-flying aircraft were sent over the occupied territories on photo-reconnaissance flights in an effort to discover troop manoeuvres. Göring's avowed intent was to knock out the RAF in four days. He had almost 3,000 aircraft at his command. Those on the French coast were within 25 minutes' striking distance of England. Operation Sea Lion seemed inevitable and imminent.

9

German fighters

At the time of the Battle of Britain the Luftwaffe was mainly using two fighter types: the Messerschmitt Bf 109 and Bf 110. The letters Bf stood for *Bayerische Flugzeugwerke,* the name of the company for which they were designed. It was not until 1938 that the company became Messerschmitt AG.

The Bf 109 was a single-seat fighter armed with two 7.9-mm machine guns on the cowling, and two 20-mm cannon in the wing roots. At the time of the Battle of Britain it was powered by a Daimler Benz DB 601 engine, though when it was first flown, in 1935, it had a Rolls-Royce Kestrel. It made its first public appearance in a fly-past during the 1936 Berlin Olympic Games. The Bf 109B and C were successfully flown in the Spanish Civil War. By August 1940 there were 23 *Gruppen* (wings) along the Channel front, mainly using the Bf 109E-3.

To give it extra lift the Bf 109 had Handley Page slats at the leading edges, connected to slotted ailerons. The engine had a fuel injector pump so the aircraft could dive steeply without the engine starving and cutting out, as happened with the Hurricane and Spitfire. But it was not as strong as those aircraft, and had to be brought out of the dive with care, for the wings had a tendency to break off under such stress. Its speed, rate of climb and dive were excellent, but it needed an experienced pilot to handle it properly. The cruising speed was 480 kmph and the maximum speed was 570 kmph. It suffered from a lack of range – 660 kilometres (not allowing for combat) – and there were no suitable long-range fuel tanks available. Its L-shaped fuel tank, on which the pilot sat, proved vulnerable, and by July 1940 armour was fitted around it, and also around the pilot's head and neck, though this cut his visibility considerably. More examples of the Bf 109, in various forms, were built than any other World War II plane, German or British: 35,000.

The Bf 110 *Zerstörer* (Destroyer) was a two-seater long-range fighter armed with four machine guns in the nose and a rear-facing machine gun operated by the crewman. It was powered by two DB 601 engines. It first flew in 1936. The Bf 110C-1 saw service in Poland in September 1939, and was used extensively in the invasion of the Low Countries and France. With a

Right: The Bf 109 and 110 were both low-wing all-metal cantilever monoplane fighters designed by Willy Messerschmitt.

cruising range of 1,100 kilometres it was intended as a bomber escort, but it was not a success and itself had to be escorted. It lacked the manoeuvrability to deal with the Hurricane and Spitfire. Built for performance, it could take little punishment and had structural weaknesses, especially around the tail. With a maximum speed of 545 kmph and a cruising speed of 460 kmph it lacked sufficient speed to be a good fighter aircraft. Evaluated as a fighter bomber during the summer of 1940, it was used increasingly in this role. Like the Bf 109, it had an L-shaped fuel tank beneath the pilot, and both types had perspex windscreens, whilst the Hurricane and Spitfire had bullet-proof glass.

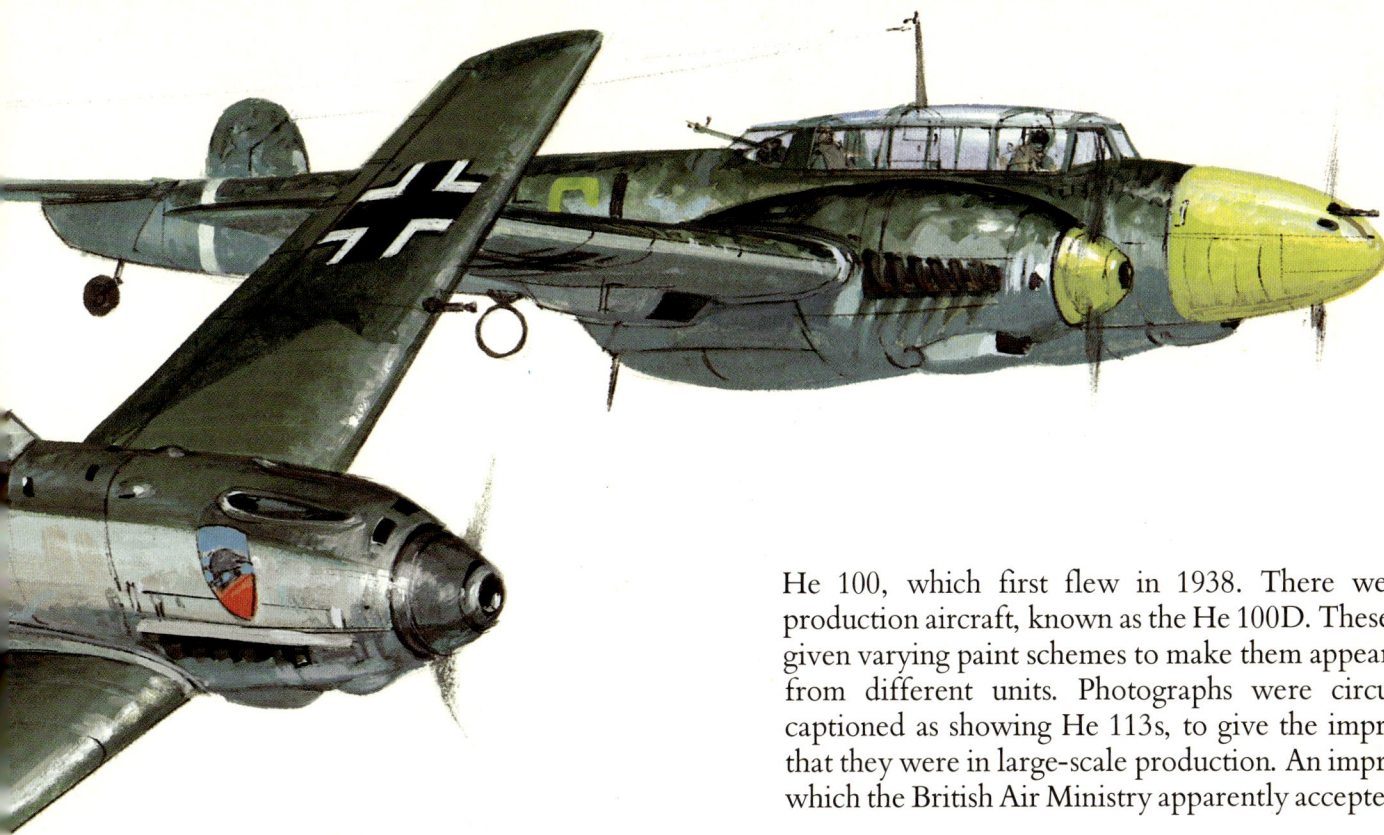

He 100, which first flew in 1938. There were 12 production aircraft, known as the He 100D. These were given varying paint schemes to make them appear to be from different units. Photographs were circulated, captioned as showing He 113s, to give the impression that they were in large-scale production. An impression which the British Air Ministry apparently accepted.

The Junkers Ju 87B Stuka (short for *Sturzkampf-flugzeug* or dive bomber) was a two-seater with a Junkers Jumo 211 engine. It had a machine gun in each wing, and a moveable machine gun in the rear cockpit. The bomb load was either one 500 kilogram bomb carried under the fuselage or one 250 kilogram bomb plus four 50 kilogram bombs under the wings. The prototype flew in 1935 and had twin tails. It crashed, and the second version had a single tail.

By the outbreak of war there were some 360 87Bs in service. It was used to clear a path before the armoured divisions in their rush across the Low Countries and France. It had a maximum speed of 370 kmph, a cruising speed of 280 kmph, and its bombing range was 600 kilometres. Its unmistakable outline, like a flattened W when seen from in front, became widely known and feared. Despite its apparent success against the evacuation of the BEF, its straight dive and pull out gave the RAF fighter pilot a steady target and, though it was used against British shipping in July and August 1940 it was used less and less over Britain.

According to an official Air Ministry account of the Battle of Britain, published in 1941, the Luftwaffe also used the Heinkel He 113 which was, stated the account, a low-wing all-metal cantilever monoplane, with a single engine, cannon firing through the airscrew hub, and two machine guns in the wings. In fact, this was the

Below: The Junkers Ju 87B was a low-wing all-metal monoplane dive bomber with a very distinctive appearance.

11

British fighters

Most of the fighters used by the RAF during the Battle of Britain were Hurricanes and Spitfires. The former was the first to fly. Designed by Sydney Camm as a successor to the Fury biplane, it was known as the Fury monoplane and was powered by a Rolls-Royce Goshawk engine.

The first Hurricane flew in October 1937, powered by a Rolls-Royce Merlin engine. In December, 111 Squadron at Northolt became the first Hurricane squadron. By the outbreak of war there were a further 17 squadrons. Because of its traditional construction – fabric over a tubular steel framework – it was a very rugged aircraft which absorbed a large amount of punishment. Production was fast: 400 were available by the outbreak of war, and 2,300 at the start of the Battle of Britain. Its wide-track undercarriage stood up to rough handling. Cockpit visibility was excellent. At 520 kmph its top speed was some 50 kmph slower than the Spitfire, and above 6,100 metres its performance deteriorated rapidly. But in partnership with the Spitfire they made a formidable team.

The Spitfire, designed by Reginald Mitchell, was a direct descendant of his brilliant seaplane designed to

Right: The Supermarine Spitfire was a single-seat all-metal cantilever monoplane fighter with similar armament to the Hurricane. Both were powered by Rolls-Royce Merlins.

Left: The Boulton and Paul Defiant was a two-seater all-metal low-wing cantilever monoplane fighter. It had four Browning machine-guns in its power-operated turret which could also be rotated manually.

Above: The Hawker Hurricane was a single-seat monoplane fighter armed with eight Browning machine-guns, four in each wing.

compete for the Schneider Trophy. The prototype flew in March 1936. In July 1938, 19 Squadron at Duxford became the first Spitfire squadron, and at the time of the Battle there were 19 such squadrons. By the end of 1939, 400 had been built with 2,000 on order. It was lighter, had a better rate of climb and, with a top speed of 570 kmph, was faster than the Hurricane. It was highly manoeuvrable, although the Bf 109 had a smaller turning circle. As the aircraft was nose-high on the ground the pilot zigzagged to see where he was going. When there was sufficient speed to lift the tail the visibility was excellent.

The Defiant first flew in August 1937 and 264 Squadron at Manston became the first Defiant squadron. It first saw action at Dunkirk where, by May 31, it had shot down 65 enemy aircraft. It had a top speed of 490 kmph and it transpired that the enemy pilots were mistaking it for a Hurricane, attacking from the rear, and were met with heavy gunfire from the turret. They learned their mistake, attacked from below, and there were such heavy losses that the Defiant was withdrawn from front-line service.

Equipped with radar it became a successful night fighter.

The Bristol Blenheim owed its birth to private enterprise. In 1935 Lord Rothermere, proprietor of the *Daily Mail,* asked the Bristol Aeroplane Company to design a twin-engined high-speed civil transport aircraft. The resulting Type 142 first flew in April 1935. It proved such an excellent machine that Rothermere presented it to the nation. This light bomber was faster than any of the then current RAF fighters. A number of Blenheims Mk IFs were ordered as fighters and had a top speed of 420 kmph. Some of the machines were converted into night fighters and AI (Airborne Interception) radar installed.

Other aircraft came under the control of Fighter Command during the Battle, when there was a desperate shortage of men and machines. The Grumman Martlet was the only American-designed aircraft to fly in the Battle. The first two machines reached Britain in August 1940 and 804 Squadron of the Fleet Air Arm (FAA), which came under the command of 13 Group, started to re-equip with Martlets in October. It was modified to British specifications, had a bullet-proof windscreen and armour plate, and four Browning guns in the wings. Its top speed was 520 kmph.

The Fairey Fulmar was first delivered to 806 Squadron FAA at Worthy Down in June 1940, and during the Battle was used by 808 Squadron FAA at Wick. The Gloster Gladiator first flew in September 1934. It was powered by a Bristol Mercury IX engine and armed with four Browning machine guns. During the Battle, 247 Squadron Gladiators defended Plymouth docks, and Sea Gladiators were used by 804 Squadron FAA. It was the only biplane fighter used by the RAF during the Battle.

Training

In Britain there was a network of establishments specially for instruction. The Central Flying School (CFS), started in 1912, instructed the instructors. As a result, instructors from the CFS would visit the Flying Training Schools to check on teachers and pupils. The RAF College, Cranwell, took cadets, mainly straight from public schools, for a two-year course to teach flying, engineering, and to become an officer. Cadets had to pay £100 per year plus £100 for their uniform and books, and were paid 6/6d (32½p) per day.

Though managed by the RAF, the University Air Squadrons were more like flying clubs than RAF squadrons. Taught to fly on Avro 504N and Tutor biplanes, at airfields near the university, students would attend summer camp at a service airfield. There were other "part-time fliers": the Special Reserve and the Auxiliary Air Force (AAF) squadrons. These fulfilled the wish of Air Chief Marshal Sir Hugh Trenchard, "the Father of the RAF", for a reserve force on territorial army lines. Often the men of the AAF were experienced sports fliers. They were officer pilots, and were taught ground trades such as fitting, rigging etc. The first enemy plane shot down over Britain during the war fell to the AAF, and 14 of the 66 squadrons which took part in the Battle of Britain were AAF squadrons.

The Air Force Volunteer Reserve was founded in 1936, for 18-25 year-olds to learn to fly at weekends free, and attend compulsory evening classes on allied subjects during the week. There were Technical Colleges to train ground crews and Halton Apprentice School, created by Trenchard, which took boys straight from secondary school for three years intensive technical training. The Air Defence Cadet Corps recruited 14-18 year-old boys. They attended three meetings a week for 3d (about 1½p), and learned the elements of flying, aircraft engineering etc.

Almost all flying training was on biplanes. Even when the Hurricane and Spitfire came into service there were no trainer versions and the Miles Magister, the standard advanced trainer between 1938 and 1942, was still used. There were flight simulators in use, and to learn to fly using instruments alone, "blind flying" hoods were fixed to the aircraft.

There was no pre-war operational training. Simulated battles at air shows and the regular Air Exercises were the nearest the pilots came to "war games". Pilots flew in tight formations. These were effective for the air show crowds, but made the pilots concentrate so hard on their positioning that they could spare no time to look for enemy aircraft.

The Germans had the best training of all; organized operational experience for men and machines before the outbreak of war. But first a "secret" air force had to be built up. The number of German service personnel permitted to fly was restricted in number under the 1926 Paris Air Agreement. So they were trained in civil flying schools. Lufthansa, the German airline, supplied

Right: University Air Squadron trainee pilots studying map navigation on the wing of one of their trainer biplanes.

Above: The Focke-Wulf Fw 56A advanced trainer, a development of the Fw 56 *Stösser* (Hawk), was designed by Kurt Tank and first flew in November 1933.

Below: The Miles Magister came into service in October 1937 and was the RAF's first monoplane basic trainer. The 'blind flying' hood can be seen here in position.

men and training facilities in the *Deutsche Verkehrsflieger Schule* (German Air Transport School).

By special arrangement with the Russians, secret military flying schools were set up there. Sports flying was enthusiastically encouraged, as was gliding, and apprentices in the civil aircraft manufacturing industry were required to build and fly a glider as part of their training. The fact that Göring, a Great War flying ace, was Hitler's deputy, added impetus to the flying training. In 1935 Hitler took from "hiding" an air force of over 1,800 machines and 20,000 men.

As far as the newly-formed Luftwaffe was concerned, the ideal training ground was the Spanish Civil War, which started in the summer of 1936. Here men discovered what life was like under battle conditions, offensive and defensive flying methods were thought out, and many machines were improved after their performance in battle had been observed. Thus, at the outbreak of war in the autumn of 1939 the Luftwaffe, then the world's youngest air force, was also the most experienced in modern air warfare.

Uniforms and equipment

Above: The German pilots are wearing two-piece leather flying suits and flying boots. The one on the left is adjusting his self-inflating life-jacket.
Below: German helmet and shatter-proof goggles.

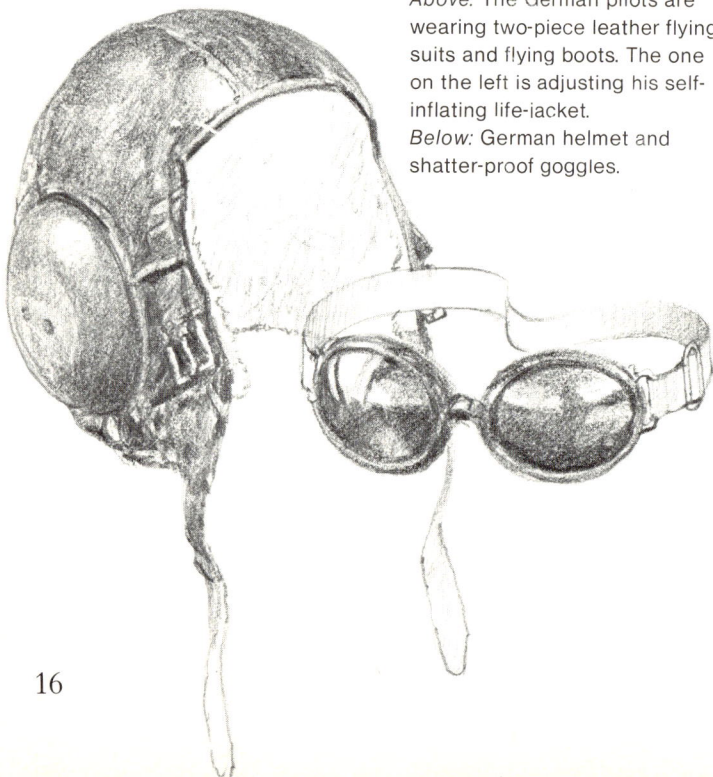

The familiar blue-grey uniform of the RAF, originally known as French blue, was referred to by members of rival services as faded blue. Officer rank was shown on the tunic cuff, and on the shoulder straps of the greatcoat and shirts. Other ranks wore their rank badges on both upper sleeves.

RAF clothing consisted of fleecy-lined leather boots, leather gauntlets, plus a pair of silk gloves and a pair of chamois leather gloves, Irvin flying suits with fleecy-lined leather jacket, leather helmet and goggles. On top of this was the Mae West life-jacket with its kapok stuffing and halter-like collar and the parachute pack, on which the pilot sat. The seat was hollowed to take the pack, which had a layer of foam rubber on it for comfort. Once in the aircraft the pilot was strapped in tightly by the Sutton Harness, which went over his shoulders and around his waist, meeting in a quick release button which had to be turned and then hit for release. Adjusting his goggles and clipping on his oxygen supply, the pilot was ready for take-off.

Comfort was very important. Pilots took to wearing silk scarves to alleviate the rub of the collar as they looked around for enemy aircraft. Woollen socks, usually home-made, were worn inside the boots, but sometimes the pilot preferred to wear shoes, although boots would support the ankle when baling out over land and were useful receptacles for maps. The thick gloves took most of the sensitivity from the pilot's hands and so the thinner chamois gloves or mittens were worn. Fire was a potential hazard, and many pilots wore overalls, which were, ostensibly, fire retarding. And for this reason many made sure there was as little uncovered skin as possible. Goggles were of great importance and some pilots, if they had the means to do so, would buy their own. Non-regulation clothing gave the pilots the look of latter-day cavaliers.

The Germans also felt that goggles were of great importance, and they were issued with either plain or tinted glass. There were three basic types of flying suits: one for summer wear, one for winter, and one for winter flying over the sea. The first was a one-piece

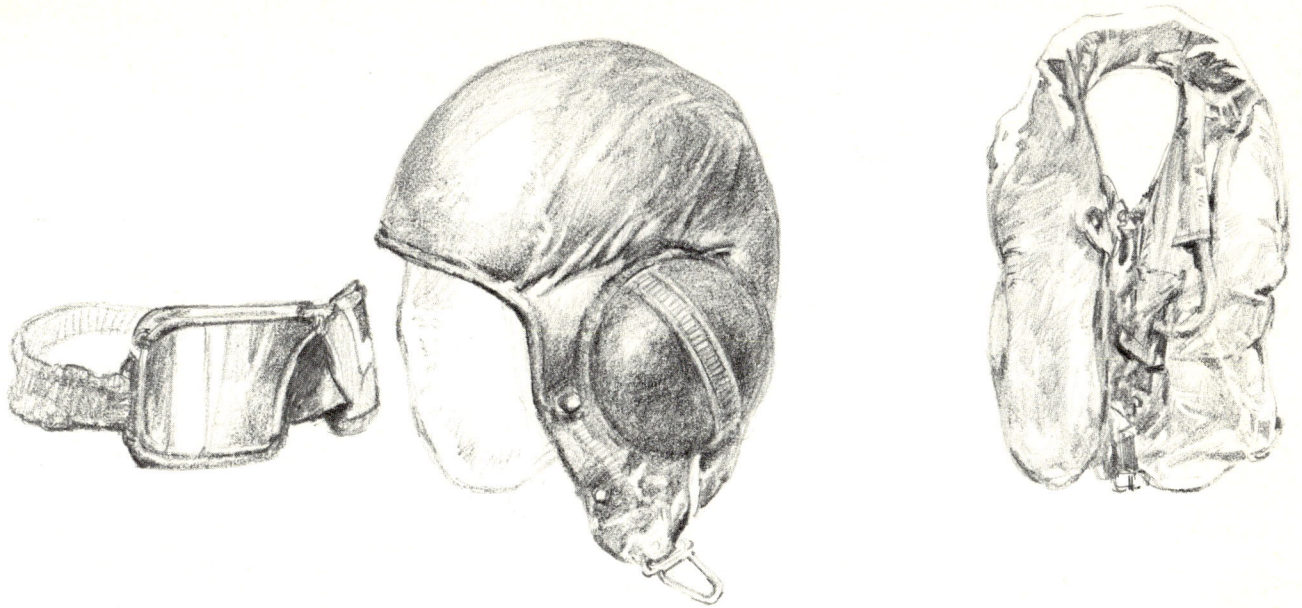

Above: British helmet, goggles and Mae West life-jacket.

Below: Three British pilots. The man in the centre is wearing a Sidcot suit, the others have flying suits with Mae West's on top. Some pilots chose to fly in shoes rather than flying boots.

overall of heavy-duty tan-coloured cotton. The second, known as the "Bulgarian Suit", was similar in design but of dark blue-grey material, with helmet, gloves and boots all of fleece-lined leather. The third was a two-piece fleece-lined leather suit in black or dark brown. Wind-cheaters were popular, though not officially issued.

The *Tuchbrock* (tunic) and *Fliegerbluse* (flying service blouse) were worn by all Luftwaffe personnel. They were of blue-grey wool and rayon mixture, or gabardine. The former was a jacket, with four box-pleated patch pockets and four metal buttons. The latter was intended for use by aircrew and so had nothing which might catch on projections in the aircraft: no cuffs, no pockets, and fly-buttoned. Blue-grey shirts, with rolled up sleeves and open collars were often worn for summer flying.

The Germans were very conscious that every flight over Britain and back meant two flights over the sea. They wore a life jacket which finished just below the waist. It was bulky and took up a lot of room in a fighter, and towards the end of 1940 it was being replaced by a life jacket similar to the Mae West. A Mauser flare pistol would be carried – usually strapped to the life jacket for safety, and the flare cartridges would often be strapped around the legs for convenience.

Both air forces share the liking for knocking the "newness" out of their hats, presumably so no-one would suspect them of being anything but experienced pilots with many flying hours in their log books.

Radar and Observer Corps

Below: A radar operator anxiously waiting for the tell-tale 'blips' of an enemy aircraft formation to come up on the screen.

The word radar was first used in America as an abbreviation for Radio Detection and Ranging, and did not come into general use until 1943. Until then RDF (Radio Direction Finding) and, subsequently, Radio Location was used.

In Britain, in 1935, a committee was set up for the scientific survey of aerial defence. Heading the committee was Henry Tizard, a physicist. He consulted Robert Watson-Watt, then superintendent of the National Physical Laboratory's Radio Research Station. Watson-Watt felt that it was important to locate the potential enemy. It was well known that aircraft interfered with radio signals, and he had the idea of locating an aircraft by radio waves.

Basically, radio energy pulses would be radiated in all directions. The pulse would strike the aircraft, and part of the pulse would rebound and be picked up by the receiver. It was realized that, in bad weather, a pilot might not find his target even though directed to the area by ground radar, and work started on making a set small enough to fit an aircraft. The result was AI (Airborne Interception).

Blenheim fighters were equipped with AI and there were six squadrons of them in operation by April 1940.

Below: Radar towers of Chain Home, Dover, standing on the white cliffs, monitoring the presence of two Messerschmitt Bf 110s.

By early 1939, radar stations to form Chain Home (CH) were being built along the east and south coasts. With three 100-metre lattice towers carrying the transmitter and four 70-metre towers carrying the receiver aerials they were impossible to hide. That May the *Graf Zeppelin* airship hovered near the east coast ·stations, which went off the air for security reasons but were still able to monitor the airship's radio messages to its home base. To catch low-flying aircraft, which could have avoided CH, Chain Home Low (CHL) was developed. This had a rotating beam, rather like a lighthouse. At first, muscle power rotated the aerial array.

Identification Friend or Foe (IFF) was developed in 1939. A transmitter in the aircraft returned a coded pulse so that it could be identified on the screen but, by early July 1940, there was still over 30 per cent of operational RAF aircraft without it. When the Battle of Britain started there was an electronic fence around Britain of 21 CH and 30 CHL stations. Apart from gaps to the west on part of the Welsh coast, the Bristol Channel and the north-west of Scotland, the barrier was 160 kilometres wide, and went up to 10,000 metres high, and all backed by the Observer Corps.

The Observer Corps, which, deservedly, became Royal in 1941, began in World War I when police reported to the Admiralty on aircraft seen and heard. By 1924 it had been realized that the whole population could be affected by air raids, and that a warning system was essential. Major-General E.B. Ashmore, who was in charge of London's air defences, organized experiments in Kent whereby groups of observation posts were linked by direct telephone line to a centre which was in turn linked to the air defence headquarters. The idea was successfully tested in the 1925 Air Exercises.

Most of the members were unpaid civilians, with a small nucleus of full-time paid officers. Some posts would be situated some way from the nearest habitation, whilst others might be on the roof of a city building. At the post would be a table, telephone, binoculars and an instrument for measuring the height and bearing of an aircraft, plus the vital equipment for brewing tea. Once the enemy aircraft was over the coastal radar it was up to the observers to report its course. Observers not only reported the height and strength of the enemy formation, but the aircraft types.

Most of the observers were aviation enthusiasts. When mobilized, the Observer Corps had 32 centres, over 1,000 posts and about 30,000 observers.

Early warning radar could detect aircraft 80 kilometres away. At a cruising speed of 300 kmph,· this meant 15-20 minutes warning. Had it not been for the radar, patrols would have had to be airborne all day in the hope of intercepting enemy aircraft. And radar could give the all-clear signal.

The Germans were ahead of the British with radar. In 1937 the *Graf Spee* had gun-ranging RDF, and by 1938 they had *Freya*, a mobile apparatus for plotting air and sea targets from the coast. It was a *Freya* at Wissant, near Calais, which located British shipping and directed the aircraft of *Erprobungsgruppe* 210 or armed speed boats to the attack. However, it could not show altitude. *Freya* on Wangerooge and Heligoland had detected the RAF raid of the winter of 1939–40 and thus contributed to their great losses. *Würzburg*, which had been demonstrated in 1939, was mainly used to guide flak *(Fliegerabwehrkanonen)* anti-aircraft guns. It could give both height and bearing.

Where the British radar won over the German was the way in which the information gained was interpreted and used.

Below: Three members of the Observer Corps take a sig'ting on an enemy formation.

19

Fighter control

Fighter Command divided the country into four main groups: No. 10 under Air Vice-Marshal (AVM) Sir Christopher Brand, with his headquarters at Box in Wiltshire, No. 11 under AVM Keith Park with his HQ at Uxbridge, Middlesex, No. 12 under AVM Trafford Leigh-Mallory at Watnall, Nottingham, and No. 13 under AVM Richard Saul at Ponteland, Newcastle-upon-Tyne. Each group was divided into sectors. Each sector contained a main fighter station and one or more satellite airfields. Each sector HQ had its own operations room and direction finding station linked to it.

From the early days of radar stations it had been realized that two neighbouring stations would report on the same enemy aircraft, which would result in a confused picture. So Filter Rooms came into being where an expert would examine the plots from all the stations, filter out duplications and send a "cleaned up" report to the operations centre. It was Watson-Watt who had first suggested that women of the Auxiliary Air Force (WAAFs) be trained as radar supervisors.

After the simplified pictures left the Filter Room they went to Fighter Command HQ Operations Room at Bentley Priory, Stanmore, Middlesex. Here was a display table showing the whole of Britain and the approaches. Long-handled magnetic-headed croupier rakes were used to move the counters representing the aircraft movements across the table. At group ops rooms the Observer Corps reports, collated at their Horsham HQ, were added. In Command HQ they had the picture for the whole country, in group and sector they had only their own area shown on the display table. In the Group HQ was a board, known as the Tote Board, on which was shown the availability and state of readiness of the squadrons under the command of that group, and it was at group that the "scramble" (take-off) was instigated.

It was the sector controller who guided the aircraft to their target once they were airborne, using radio telephone. He was always someone with flying experience, so he could more readily visualize what was happening at the receiving end of his messages. From the blip on the radar screen to the pilot running to his aircraft, only six minutes elapsed. It can be understood from this how vital were the direct-link telephone lines used. The ops rooms at Bentley Priory and No. 11 and No. 12 Group HQs were the only ones housed in concrete bunkers. The rest were all above ground and vulnerable.

The RAF operations room was rather like an operating theatre. There was a large table, and a gallery where vitally interested personnel sat. The table was a large-scale map, and around it sat the WAAFs, each wearing a head set, with a long rake in her hand. As she received information so she would move relevant counters on the table with her rake. A clock, common in style to, and synchronised with, clocks in all the ops rooms, was divided into five minute sections, each section having a different colour: red, yellow and blue repeated. As the hands moved to a new colour, so all the fresh counters used would be of the corresponding colour. Thus a controller could tell at a glance how fresh was the plot he was observing from the gallery. It was seldom more than four minutes out, or the equivalent of about 25 kilometres for the aircraft represented on the table.

The German chain of command was somewhat different. At the top was the Combined High Command (*Oberkommando der Wehrmacht – OKW*) and then the Luftwaffe High Command (*Oberkommando der*

Left: The five-minute colour change clock can be clearly seen in this view of the Filter Room at Bentley Priory.

Above: The ops room at Bentley Priory, showing the WAAFs using their long-handled rakes to move the counters across the table, and the viewing gallery above.

Luftwaffe - OKL). Next came the *Luftflotten.* Each *Luftflotte* was designated an area and its strength, varying from 200 to 1,300 aircraft, depended on the importance of that area. *Luftflotte 2* was commanded by *Generalfeldmarschall* Albert Kesselring from his HQ in Brussels, and covered Holland, Belgium and north-east France. *Luftflotte 3,* in north-west France, was commanded by *Generalfeldmarschall* Hugo Sperrle, with his HQ in Paris. *Luftflotte 5,* in Scandinavia, was commanded by *Generaloberst* Hans-Jürgen Stumpff from his HQ in Stavanger. Next in the chain of command came the *Fliegerdivision,* or *Fliegerkorps* as it later became. Again, the number of aircraft could vary between 200 and 750. A *Geschwader* (group) was usually made up of 90 aircraft in three *Gruppen* (wings), each *Gruppe* usually comprised 27 aircraft in three *Staffeln* (squadrons), and each *Staffel* was composed of nine aircraft.

The German ops room resembled a cinema in that it had a screen, tiered seats and projectionists. The screen was a large, translucent map. In the tiers of seats facing it sat the officers, each in constant touch with an airfield. In a seat at the back of the stalls sat the Chief Operations Officer. Behind the screen sat the projectionists. They were the *Luftwaffenhelferinen* (German WAAFs) who projected onto the map the current state of affairs. They used a torch-like projector into which was fitted a filter so that various symbols could be shown on the screen. The ops rooms were built in massive bomb-proof concrete bunkers.

Kanalkampf

In his "Directive 16" Hitler had said that the preparation for Operation Sea Lion should be completed by mid-August. Before the invasion could take place, Britain's maritime life-line must be cut and her naval forces neutralized. Most of her vital supplies arrived by sea. Comparatively few merchant ships were equipped with Asdic (underwater radar). At this time the merchantmen did not form into mutually-protective convoys in the Atlantic, and so were easy prey to the U-boats, even though the submarines did not form "wolf packs" until September 1940. In June alone 300,000 tonnes of shipping was lost to U-boats. But the chief concern of the Germans at this time was to make the Channel safe for their proposed invasion.

The Channel had to be cleared. Two *Fliegerkorps* were assigned to this duty: No. II from Pas de Calais and No. VII from Le Havre. *Oberst* Johannes Fink was given the title *Kanalkampfführer* (Channel Battle Leader). In all he had about 75 bombers, 60 Stukas and 200 fighters under his command. His command post was an old bus on the cliffs at Cap Blanc Nez, parked near the statue commemorating the famous cross-channel flight of Louis Bleriot in 1909.

July was a mainly wet and cloudy month, but every day from July 10 to the first week in August the Luftwaffe launched attacks on shipping and/or harbours, and did much mine laying. Ships are usually easy to spot. However well camouflaged, nothing can hide the white wake pointing directly to them.

CH and CHL could not give early enough warniong of enemy aircraft approaching when they had to be intercepted over the sea. To cross the Channel took five minutes, but the RAF fighters needed 15 minutes to gain operational height. So from July 4, standing patrols had to be mounted. A flight from each forward sector base would patrol and radio if they spotted "bandits". Help would be some time arriving and so the patrols would often attack, although heavily outnumbered.

Dowding warned the Air Staff and the Admiralty that he did not have sufficient fighters to protect shipping as well as defend Britain and, despite heavy pressure, especially from the navy, he used his resources sparingly. The patrols and the defence of the shipping was a great drain on those resources. If the fighters protected the shipping, then some must be lost. If they stayed on the ground, then the shipping must be lost. Nevertheless, Dowding resisted the temptation to strengthen the south-eastern sectors, realizing that this would put him in a position where he could be outflanked. Instead, he strengthened those flanks.

Late in July the *Freya* at Wissant came into operation, and was able to guide torpedo boats and aircraft to the convoys. Stukas were used to attack shipping, especially in the Channel, despite the fact that the convoys flew barrage balloons to discourage low-level attacks.

Left: Junkers Ju 87 'Stukas' start their steady diving attack on Dover Harbour, despite being attacked by British fighters.

Although unrivalled for precision bombing the Stuka was one of the easiest aircraft to shoot down, for by the time it was diving on its target it had outstripped its fighter escort, and as it dived and pulled up in a straight line it presented a steady target. Flying low over the sea was very difficult, and more than one pilot was lost because he found it impossible to judge his height above the waves.

By the first week in August the Straits of Dover were so dangerous that hardly a ship passed through them. Destroyers were withdrawn, and much of the naval force was drawn back from the area of maximum danger. This did at least afford the fighters some rest. On August 8 there was a battle involving about 200 aircraft, with three major attacks on a convoy. The result was 31 Luftwaffe machines lost for 19 RAF. German intelligence interpreted this to show that it was Fighter Command's last stand. In less than a month *Kanalkampfführer* Fink had apparently won the air supremacy over the Dover Straits. And rationing in Britain became a way of life.

Bombers and tactics

Apart from the Ju 87 Stuka there were three bomber types used by the Luftwaffe at this time. The Dornier Do 17 was familiarly known as the "Flying Pencil". It had two Brama 323 engines, and was armed with two forward-firing machine guns, but this was increased by adding one dorsal, one ventral, and two through side windows. During the Battle two further free-mounted machine guns were added. Its speed was about 365 kmph, but this increased as it would approach its target in a shallow dive. Originally ordered as a fast mail plane for Lufthansa, it first flew in 1934. Rejected as having insufficient passenger space, it was developed into a fast light bomber. The Do 215 was a development of the Do 17, and had a crew of four or five and was powered by two DB 601 engines.

The Junkers Ju 88A–1 had two Jumo 211B engines and could reach 520 kmph. The prototype flew in December 1936, just 11 months after the design work had started. In 1938 production started, and some were in service by the outbreak of war.

The Heinkel He 111P had the DB 601A engines, but the He 111H, the definitive model in 1939, had two less powerful Jumo 211A, the superior Daimler Benz engines being allotted to the Bf 109. It was armed with movable machine guns in the nose, on top of the fuselage and in the blister below. Originally envisaged as an airliner its potential as a bomber was obvious. The

prototype was completed in 1935 and went into mass production. After service in the Spanish Civil War it was equipped with a glazed nose section.

Bombers needed to be protected by fighters, but the latter were faster and had a shorter range. There were, therefore, many tactics devised to protect the bombers, and to attack them. An obvious idea was to send fighters to engage the RAF fighters then, just as the RAF were having to break off to refuel, the bombers would arrive. But the RAF had instructions to go for only the bombers. So Luftwaffe fighters tried flying in bomber formation. The blips picked up by radar could not distinguish the type of aircraft, the RAF scrambled only to be met by fighters instead of the expected bombers.

German fighters were also instructed to mix with the bombers, but this was not popular as it robbed them of the two advantages they needed to attack fighters: speed and height. Using fighters to scout ahead of the bomber force, others to accompany them to the target and relief by other fighters on their return used a lot of aircraft and was not successful. Another method was to have fighters above and on either side of the bombers. When one section was attacked, that section would break from the bombers to give battle, their place being taken by the fighters above, whose place in turn would be taken by those flying on the other side of the formation.

It was important to break up the bomber formation in order to attack them. No. 111 Squadron would line their Hurricanes abreast and charge the formation, forcing them to scatter. It was also important that the RAF fighters be scrambled early enough to reach operational height (about 20 minutes). With the enemy approaching at 320 kmph the fighters at coastal airfields

Left: The Dornier Do 17 was a high-wing all-metal cantilever monoplane bomber with a crew of three.

did not have time to get the height advantage. Squadron Leader Bader's "Big Wing" was something which No. 12 Group could manage. Being further north they had time to get three squadrons airborne to the right height at the right time. It was important to get height, and to attack from the sun if possible.

At 8,500 metres the grease on the guns could freeze. Fabric patches over the gun barrel openings prevented this and stayed in position until the first burst of fire. If boots were wet when getting into the plane the soles could freeze to the rudder bar. Cut potato rubbed on the windscreen stopped it frosting up, but many pilots, terrified of fire and of being unable to get out in time, would lock their cockpit hood open, despite the cold.

British fighters, with their lack of operational training, still tended to fly in the tight formations admired by pre-war air show crowds. The Germans had developed the *schwarm* (swarm), later to be adopted by the RAF as "finger four" because of the positioning of the four aircraft in a loose arc, at different altitudes, all able to guard their neighbour's tail but with little likelihood of collision.

Many RAF pilots had little or no gunnery practice. They tended to fire when still out of range and break off when they should have commenced firing, or peel off after firing to expose their underside to the bomber's guns instead of breaking under the bomber. The pressure of the gun button on the stick could push the nose down, and so the stick had to be steadied with one hand while the other pressed the button. Bomber Command felt that the combined fire from a formation of bombers would be enough to see off fighters. But the Luftwaffe fighters were armed with cannon which had a longer range than the bombers' machine guns.

Right: The Junkers Ju 88 was a four-seater monoplane with movable machine guns in the nose, on top of the fuselage, and in the blister below.

Above: The insignia of JG 3.
Left: A Bf 109 rudder showing the pilot's 'kills'.

Heraldry

The swastika is a very old device. It has been used by ancient civilizations from Mexico to Tibet, and from Peru to Greece. It was only after the Great War that the symbol became associated with anti-Semitism and became the emblem of the Nazi party that it fell into disrepute.

Germans often marked their aircraft with their squadron insignia, for example ace of spades, dragons, or a variety of devils, eagles and lions. Individuals also had their own insignia. *Generalleutnant* Adolf Galland had Mickey Mouse waving a gun and hatchet and smoking a cigar. Another Walt Disney character, Figaro the Cat, decorated Squadron Leader Ian Gleed's Hurricane. Pilot Officer D. du Vivier, a Belgian with 43 Squadron, flew a Hurricane decorated with the crossed flags of Belgium and the RAF. Flight Lieutenant Johnny Kent, a Canadian flying in a Polish squadron, decorated his machine with a white Polish eagle on a green maple leaf. The Cross of Lorraine, adopted as the emblem of the Free French movement during the war, appeared on the aircraft piloted by those Frenchmen who had managed to escape from France.

Family crests and drawings which made a play of the pilot's name or nickname were popular, as were horseshoes, four-leafed clovers, black cats, playing cards and other good luck signs. Shark's teeth were painted on aircraft of the *Haifisch gruppe.*

When the war began, the Ministry of Aircraft Production announced that the nominal cost of a Hurricane or Spitfire was £5,000. This had patriotic groups, even individuals, subscribing to buy an aircraft. Such presentation machines would bear a name to show who had donated them, such as "City of Warwick". By August 1940 the Commonwealth had donated 40 bombers and 60 fighters.

Girls named Dorothy bought a Spitfire and named it "Dorothy of Great Britain and the Empire". Redheads bought a Spitfire and named it "Gingerbread". It was even flown by a redhead. But possibly the best-known of the presentation aircraft were those given by Lady MacRobert. One of her sons was killed in a civil accident before the war, and two others were killed during the war. She bought four Hurricanes, three of which were named after her dead sons.

There were two Polish fighter squadrons in the Battle: 302 and 303. The former, based at Duxford, was formed mainly of pilots from the Polish Air Force squadrons based in Poznan. The 302 Squadron adopted the crow emblem and became known as The City of Poznan Fighter Squadron. Whereas 303 Squadron, based at Northolt, had most of its pilots from the crack 111 Squadron of the Polish Air Force which had been formed from the No. 7 Kosciuszko Squadron. The squadron adopted as their badge a peasant's hat of the Cracow district, crossed with two long-handled scythes of the type used by the peasants in their fight against the Russians in the 18th century. In the background were the American stars and stripes, recalling the part played by Tadeusz Kosciuszko in the American War of Independence. But it was the large bare surfaces of bombers that lent themselves so readily to insignia.

Below: A Bf 109 of *Jagdgeschwader* (fighter group) 26. Their emblem was the Red Griffin (shown).

Adler Angriff (Eagle Attack)

With the Channel emptied of British shipping, the RAF became the next target. The tall towers of the coastal radar could be seen from France. The Luftwaffe's monitoring service had been listening to the radio signals put out by the RAF and had come to the conclusion that they were connected with the towers. These radar stations had to be wiped out before the RAF could be destroyed. If they remained in operation there could be no surprise attacks. Immediately after the radar stations had been neutralized, attacks could be made on coastal fighter stations. At the same time pressure would also be kept up on naval targets. This attack, code-named *Adler Angriff* (Eagle Attack), was to be followed the next day by the main all-out attack on Britain – *Adler Tag* (Eagle Day). The meteorologists had assured Göring that the weather would be fine.

Throughout July and August *Erprobungsgruppe* (experimental group) 210 had been attacking British shipping. This task force of 28 men under *Hauptmann* Walter Rubensdörffer had been formed to evaluate the Me 210 and also the Bf 109 and 110 as fighter bombers. They were to prove that these aircraft could not only carry bombs, but use them successfully and then return to their fighter role. Their targets regarded them as relatively harmless fighters, until the bombs dropped.

Each aircraft could carry two 450 kilogram bombs (twice the bomb load of a Ju 87).

On Monday August 12 at 8.40 am, 16 aircraft of *Erprobungsgruppe* took off from Calais and crossed the Channel at an altitude of 5,500 metres. Their mission was to knock out four radar stations. They split into four sections, each composed of four Bf 110s. Each section took a target: Rye, Pevensey, Dover, and Dunkirk. At Rye all the huts were destroyed, yet the transmitting and receiving blocks were undamaged. At Pevensey the damage included a cut in the vital electricity main. At Dover the aerial towers were slightly damaged and the huts were destroyed. At Dunkirk, somewhat further inland, a 450 kilogram bomb actually shifted the concrete transmitting block some centimetres.

Dunkirk was the only station to remain on the air, and that left a gaping hole in the radar chain. This enabled the forward airfields at Hawkinge and Lympne to be hit without warning. At Hawkinge there was serious damage inflicted by Ju 88s; five men were killed, seven seriously injured, four fighters destroyed on the ground, and 28 bomb craters littered the airfield. Yet it was fully operational by the next morning. Lympne was hit by 141 bombs.

Above: Two Messerschmitt Bf 110s of *Erprobungsgruppe* 210 make a low-level attack on radar installations. Their insignia of an outline map of the British Isles in red overlain by a yellow gunsight can be seen on the fuselage.
Below: A Messerschmitt Bf 109 being loaded with a 450 kilogram bomb. The bomb rack can be seen between the landing wheels.

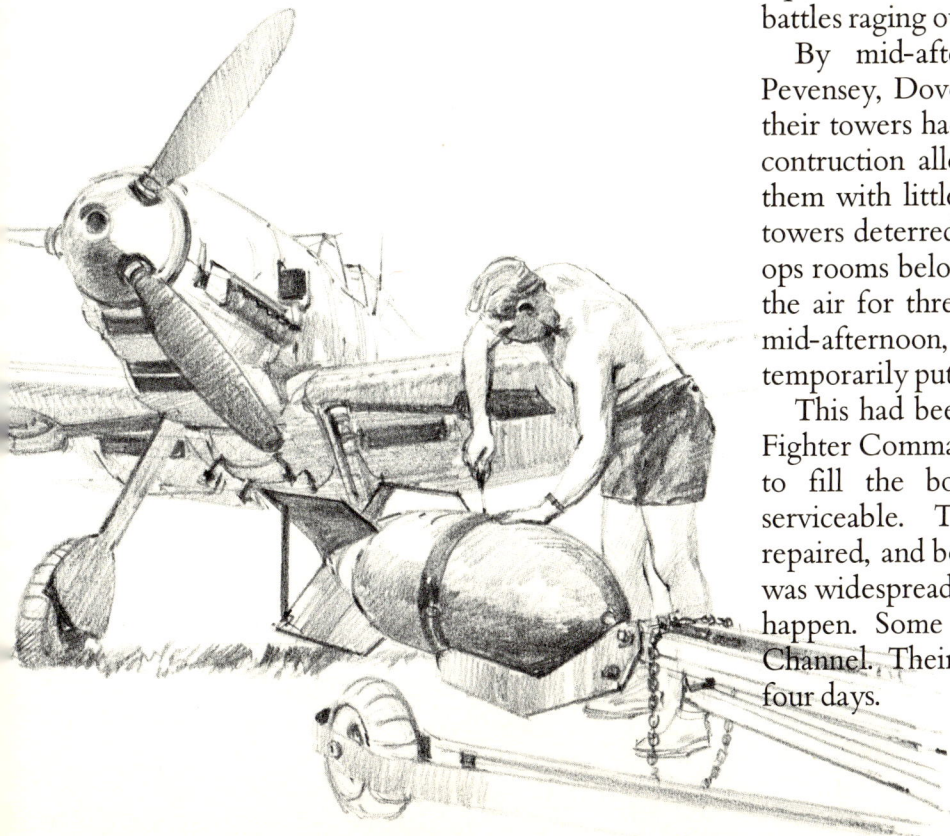

Then the task force came back with 20 Bf 109s and Bf 110s and bombed Manston before defending aircraft could get airborne. This was the first attack of many on Manston, so temptingly perched on the Kent cliff tops. Only one casualty was recorded, but the bombs made a mess of the runway and it was unserviceable for a day.

Whilst the task force was making this second sortie there was a big raid building up further along the south coast. At mid-day almost 100 Ju 88s escorted by 120 Bf 110s and 25 Bf 109s were detected by Poling radar in Sussex. This radar station had not been attacked, and reported the large formation heading for Brighton. But they then turned left and followed the coast to Spithead. There the bomber force split. Over 70 of them turned north to Portsmouth, through the gap in the balloon barrage. Every anti-aircraft gun in the area opened up at them as they made a devastating attack on the docks and town.

When they turned for home they found 213 Squadron Hurricanes waiting in ambush. About 15 bombers had turned south at Spithead and ferociously attacked the radar station at Ventnor, Isle of Wight. This force was in turn attacked by Spitfires from 152 and 609 Squadrons. AVM Park was feeding his aircraft gradually into the fray. It had become a habit for the Germans to send out fresh fighters to escort their bombers home. This ploy had not gone unnoticed, and when the relief force was sighted, Park sent up 615 Squadron Hurricanes to prevent them joining the battles raging over Spithead and the Isle of Wight.

By mid-afternoon the radar stations at Rye, Pevensey, Dover and Dunkirk were all on the air. All their towers had withstood the onslaught. Their lattice contruction allowed the bomb blasts to pass through them with little damage. Also, the very height of the towers deterred dive bombers from attacking the vital ops rooms below them. The station at Ventnor was off the air for three days. Lympne was attacked again in mid-afternoon, and the 242 bombs dropped on it temporarily put it out of service.

This had been the most intensive day's fighting for Fighter Command to date. All night long men laboured to fill the bomb craters and make the runways serviceable. Telephone and power cables were repaired, and bodies dug out of the rubble. The feeling was widespread that something very nasty was about to happen. Some 2,000 German aircraft lay across the Channel. Their mission was to wipe out the RAF in four days.

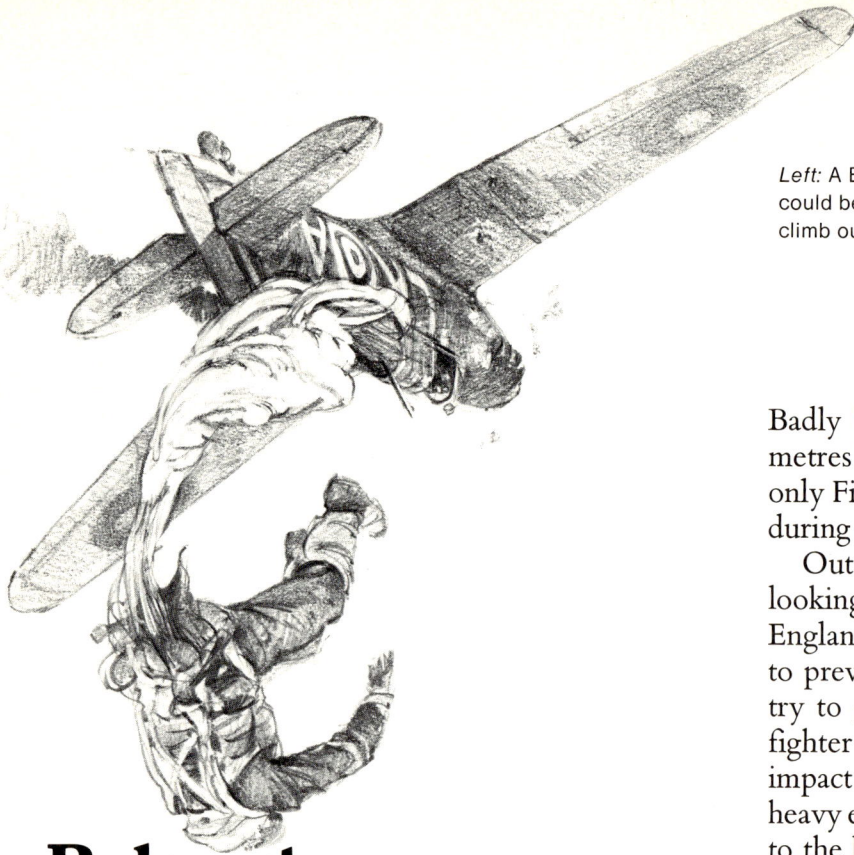

Bale out

Left: A British pilot bales out from a stricken Hurricane. If the aircraft could be inverted the pilot could simply fall out, instead of having to climb out.

A man and his machine might have to part company many times, especially if the machine were on fire or so crippled that it could not be landed safely, or had insufficient fuel to make a safe landing anywhere.

Fire was a terrifying hazard. The fuel tank was in front of RAF fighter pilots, and there was not always a fire wall to protect him. In German fighters the pilot sat on the L-shaped self-sealing fuel tank. These were treated with a rubberized compound which closed over any small hole made in them. Some pilots made sure that no bare skin was showing. Overalls were thought to be fire inhibiting. Some pilots locked their cockpit hood in the open position before combat. This meant that they could not get trapped but that they were unprotected from the weather and bullets. There are many horrific stories told of pilots in burning aircraft who could actually smell their own flesh cooking and watch their skin blistering.

Flight Lieutenant Eric James Brindley Nicolson of 249 Squadron was caught in a burning aircraft. His Hurricane was badly shot up by a Bf 110. His reserve tank was hit and caught fire, and further shots wounded his foot. The Bf 110 overshot the Hurricane and, despite the fact that the instrument panel was melting with the heat and his hands were blistering, he stayed with his aircraft and shot down the enemy aircraft.

Badly burned, he baled out and free fell for 1,500 metres before managing to pull the ripcord. He was the only Fighter Command pilot to win the Victoria Cross during the Battle.

Out of fuel, a pilot might well land on a smooth looking field, though most such places in southern England had ditches dug across them, or poles planted, to prevent the enemy landing. A German pilot would try to get back across the Channel. To try to land a fighter on the water was very risky. Apart from an impact like driving into a brick wall, the comparatively heavy engine in the nose would take the aircraft straight to the bottom, unlike a bomber which might float for two or three minutes.

So most pilots preferred to "take to the silk". The drill for parachuting into water sounds complicated, but had to be second nature to a pilot, and many an injured man was saved because of the drill which he must have carried out in a state of semi-consciousness. At about 30 metres from the water, which was very difficult to judge, he should turn the quick release button on his parachute harness. A few metres from the water he should straighten his body, feet together, elbows at his side, and pinch his nose. As his feet touched the water he should strike the quick release button, thereby releasing the parachute. If he could not get rid of the chute he could easily be dragged under the water.

There is a recorded case of a pilot who baled out of his Spitfire at 8,500 metres and timed his drop into the sea as taking 24½ minutes. He had plenty of time to remove his boots and drop them into the sea at intervals in order to judge his height above the water. But men were not always so happy to wet their boots. Flying Officer John Gibson, a New Zealander, was wearing brand new hand-made shoes when he was attacked over Folkestone. With his aircraft on fire he jettisoned his shoes, aimed the burning Hurricane out to sea, and baled out at 300 metres. Amazingly his shoes were found, posted to Hawkinge, and there rejoined their owner.

From a great height it was prudent to free fall for a while in order to reach the height where breathing was easy. The pilot relied on his oxygen mask above about

2,750 metres. This tended to give the pilot time to wonder just how reliable was his parachute, and as a result he was likely to pull the release sooner than was advisable.

There are reports of men being shot at as they hung beneath the canopy. Such incidents were not common, for the victor seldom had time to follow the vanquished. There was some justification for the Germans to shoot at RAF crewmen baling out over Britain, for they would be able to fight another day, just as German pilots baling out over France could be considered fair game. But a Luftwaffe pilot baling out over Britain might well be a source of useful information.

Much of the Battle of Britain was fought high over agricultural land, and many a farmer had an aircraft plant itself in his fields. Flight Lieutenant Johnny Kent shot down a Bf 109 from 5,000 metres. It hit the ground vertically, and the engine ended up 10 metres deep in the earth.

Below: A Luftwaffe pilot arrives in England under his silk canopy. Farm workers, armed with anything that might serve as a weapon, advance on the parachutist to discover whether he is friend or foe.

Above: A Heinkel He 59 float plane rescuing a Luftwaffe fighter crew from a dinghy.

Air-sea rescue

The RAF fighter pilot who went "down in the drink" had just two things on which to rely: his luck and his Mae West. The Mae West was a life jacket, named after the film actress. It was filled with wads of kapok, and had a halter collar which was supposed to keep his head above the water. But it had to be inflated by the wearer's own lungs, which was not easy and was sometimes impossible if the man were wounded or exhausted.

His best chance of being spotted was when he was still swinging beneath his parachute. If he could be seen then by a watcher on the shore, or by a fellow pilot who

could report his position, he might well be saved. Once in the water, he was a very small dot in a large expanse of water. Even during that summer of 1940 the sea, especially the North Sea, was cold, and exposure kills quickly. A man could not expect to remain conscious for more than two hours.

An aircraft in trouble over the sea would send out a Mayday call. When this was picked up by an RAF unit it would be passed to the Fighter Command Movement Liaison Section, who in turn passed it to the naval authorities, to Coastal Command and to coastguards. As the war hotted up, and more and more men died in

Below: One of the RAF high-speed launches.

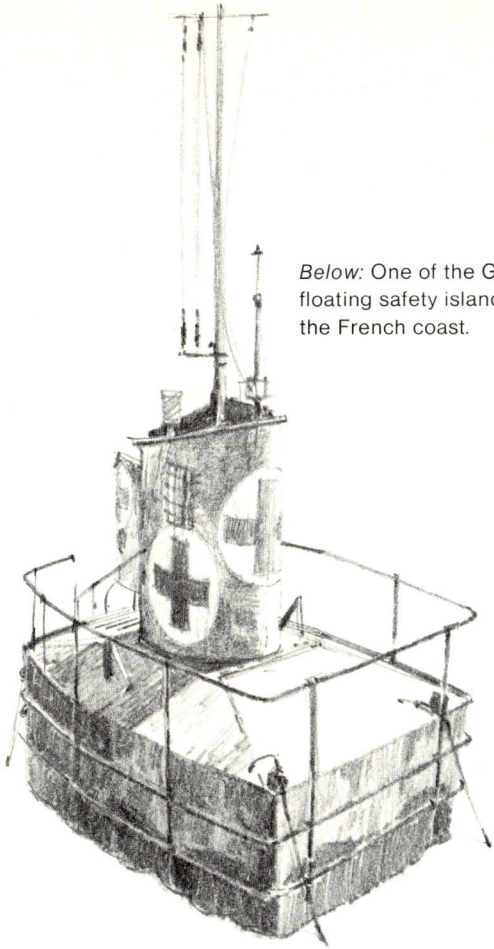

Below: One of the German floating safety islands moored off the French coast.

The Germans already had a well-organized air-sea rescue service. They used the Heinkel He 59 float plane for search and rescue. It was part of their *Seenotflugkommando* (air-sea rescue unit). Originally they bore a red cross, but after they were fired on by the RAF they were camouflaged and armed. The Air Ministry argued that men down in the sea who might get back to German bases to fight again were still in combat and they were therefore justified in shooting at them. The Luftwaffe fighter pilots and crewmen had inflatable dinghies, and also carried bags of dye with them with which to colour the sea around them. To further aid rescuers they wore yellow skull caps and scarves. They were also equipped with flares. The Germans also had safety islands, or "float boats" as they were called when the RAF eventually got around to copying the idea. These were rafts moored off the French coast and regularly checked by patrol boats to see whether anyone had sought refuge there.

the sea, it was decided that the saving of life should be given greater priority.

From July 10 (the first day of *Kanalkampf*) to the end of the month, over 200 aircrew were listed as killed or missing – most of them over the sea. So at the end of July Vice-Admiral Sir Bertram Ramsay (Vice-Admiral, Dover), and AVM Park of No. 11 Group, organized a rescue service for the much fought over south-east coast of England. They had some light naval craft, RAF high-speed launches, and some Westland Lysanders, borrowed from Army Co-Operation Command. After an engagement a Lysander, with fighter escort, would set out to search for downed men. When survivors were sighted, a dinghy, carried in the Lysander's bomb racks, would be dropped, and its position reported to base, so that a launch could be sent to pick them up. There were a mere 19 of the high-speed launches to provide rescue along the south coast, although any shipping in the area was told to look out for survivors. If the man had the strength to reach the dinghy, if the weather had not closed in so he could not be seen, and if the tide, which could reach a speed of seven knots, had not carried him too far from his reported position, then he might be rescued.

Below: A Lysander having a dinghy pack fitted to its undercarriage bomb rack.

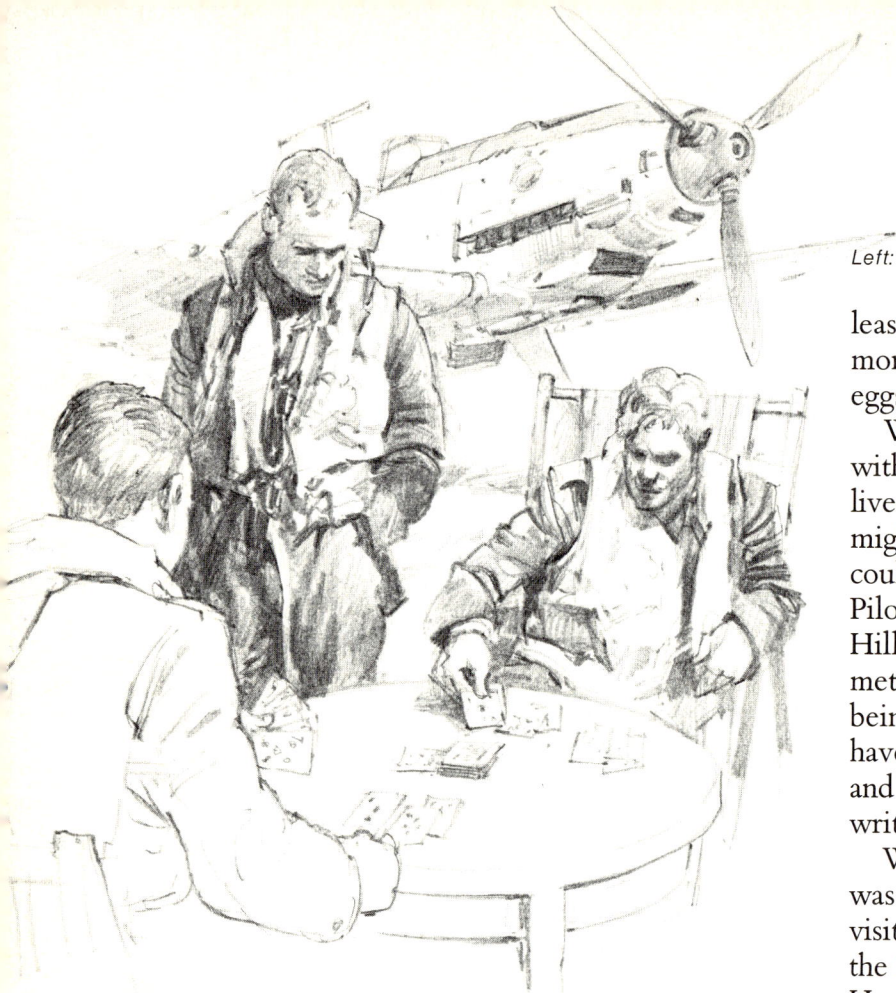

Dispersal

least the pilot's food was basically more plentiful and more varied than that available to civilians at the time; eggs were on the menu most days.

When off-duty the men might go home, if they lived within easy reach of their station. Some of those who lived further away, or those who came from overseas, might well be taken in by a local family, so that they could enjoy some sort of family life on their days off. Pilots at some of the forward airfields, such as Biggin Hill, were dispersed to a country house some kilometres from the base because of the danger of the base being bombed. No. 92 Squadron were lucky enough to have a very good pianist in Pilot Officer Bob Holland, and turned their fine new home into a night club, writing their own licensing hours.

With the airfields being sited in the country there was usually a wealth of little village inns and pubs to visit. Once such an establishment became popular with the RAF it was adopted as their club house. The White Hart at Brasted, near Biggin Hill, was an example. The RAF men who frequented it put their signatures to one of the blackboards used as a blackout shutter over a

There were three categories of readiness at Fighter Command stations: available, dispersal or readiness, and stand by or cockpit readiness. Men who were available had to be on the station and ready to take-off in 30 minutes. Those at the dispersal point had to be fully kitted out, apart from helmets and parachutes, and ready to be airborne in five minutes. Those on stand by were already in their cockpits, strapped in and ready to switch on the engine.

The station would have as many creature comforts as possible, facilities for film shows and dances, and for sports such as cricket, football, billiards and darts. There would be administrative offices, medical offices, and the hangars for the maintenance and repair of the aircraft. These were overhauled every 180 flying hours. The older flying stations – those built pre-war – were the more comfortable, being brick-built and with proper facilities. Those which had mushroomed during the war were often little more than hutted camps. At

Above: A sing-song around the piano was just one of several ways RAF pilots could relax in an evening.

Below: Pilots of 72 Squadron based at Hawkinge relax in the sunshine beside their Hurricanes.

window. This historical example of graffiti is currently in the RAF Museum at Hendon, North London.

Just as the off-duty pilots were dispersed from the airfield, so were the aircraft. Previously, the aircraft had been all lined up smartly on parade, wingtip to wingtip. But if one aircraft was hit, the chain reaction would destroy the whole line. They were therefore dispersed around the airfield in blast pens. If an aircraft was hit, the blast was prevented from reaching any aircraft in the next pen by a wall of earth or concrete.

At the dispersal point there was a room or hut furnished with half a dozen beds, easy chairs, perhaps a table-tennis table or dart board, and gramophone. There would also be the vital coal stove for dawn, by which time the point must be manned (it could be cold even in summer), and the all-important telephone. Here the pilots would relax as best they could, enjoying the sunshine, playing cards, reading or just dozing. But ready to leap into action at the shrill call of the telephone. Then they must don their helmets and run to their aircraft.

The aircraft would be facing into the wind, and with the engines warmed up every few hours by the ground crew. The pilot's parachute would usually be waiting for him on the wing. The ground crew would have been summoned by the bell, and be at the aircraft ready to help the pilot into his parachute and strap him into the cockpit, while he plugged in his wireless transmitter and oxygen, adjusted his goggles and started the engine.

On returning from a sortie the pilots would report to the Intelligence Officer to be de-briefed. He would quiz them on what they had done and what they had seen. Often important intelligence could be made from seemingly unimportant scraps of information.

At this time the Luftwaffe pilots, being on the offensive, did not have to live by the telephone. They knew their flying schedule in advance, and meanwhile they could relax and wait.

Black Thursday (August 15)

Above: Heinkel IIIs being attacked by Spitfires.

Eagle Day was due to be launched the day after Eagle Attack had bombed the radar stations and forward airfields. But because of bad weather it did not start until Thursday August 15. The attack was launched from airfields from Brittany to Norway.

The aircraft from Stavanger in Norway had the furthest to fly. Allowing for take-off, landing, finding the target, attack and navigation errors, they had some 1,600 kilometres to cover. The He 111s from *Luftflotte* 5 were therefore escorted by Bf 110s with long-range fuel tanks known as 'dachsund bellies'. These gave them an extra 1,000 litres of fuel but added so much to the load that the rear gunners were left behind. Their mission was to attack the north and north-east of England. They had been told to expect little opposition because German intelligence had presumed that Dowding had stripped the northern defences in order to strengthen the south.

This was just one of the errors which led to this catastrophic day being known in the annals of Luftwaffe history as 'Black Thursday'. Another error was caused by navigation. Before the He 111s and their escorts were due to reach England, a feint was made by two squadrons of Heinkel He 115 seaplanes. These set a course for Dundee in order to attract the defending aircraft northwards from the Edinburgh area. But the bombers flew along an almost identical course. Thus not only was the element of surprise gone but the defending forces had even more warning than was normal for air-raids.

Eventually the bombers realized their mistake and headed south to find the whole of 72 Squadron waiting for them off the Farne Islands. Some of the Bf 110s, unable to jettison their long-range tanks properly, took refuge in the 'circle of death' defensive manoeuvre in which each followed its leader and guarded his tail. The unprotected bombers broke formation, some dumping their bombs in the sea and heading for home. Others continued south to be met by 605 Squadron. Although some bombs from the raid fell on land, little damage was caused.

Further south Ju 88s from Aalborg in Denmark were intercepted off the Yorkshire coast by only 18 aircraft from 12 Group. The bombers were thus able to successfully bomb Driffield, a Bomber Command base, and 10 Whitley bombers were destroyed on the ground.

Meanwhile, to the south, Hawkinge was severely attacked. Worse still, the main electricity cable was cut which put the Dover and Rye CH and Foreness CHL stations out of action. Lympne and Manston were also hit again. In mid-afternoon Martlesham Heath was attacked and put out of action; it was not completely operational for 48 hours. Short's factory at Rochester was attacked and six Stirlings destroyed. Eastchurch, Middle Wallop, Worthy Down, Odiham, and Portland naval base were all raided. In the early evening it was the turn of West Malling and Croydon. At night it was Beverley, Birmingham, Bristol, Boston, Crewe, Harwich, Southampton, Swansea, and Yarmouth.

But the Germans met opposition everywhere. Their losses were far heavier than had been anticipated (75 German aircraft were lost for 34 RAF). The Bf 110 had proved unsuitable as an escort and itself needed to be escorted. Stukas were also to have a heavier escort in future. Each wing would have three fighter wings to protect them. One wing would stay with them as they dived, a second wing would fly ahead and scout defences, while a third would protect the formation from above. From the 120 fighters needed, some had to be kept in reserve for the flight back over the Channel. This was going to severely deplete the Luftwaffe's fighter force. And as it appeared that the attacks on radar installations were not having any effect, Göring saw little point in continuing with these raids.

All day Churchill had been at Fighter Command HQ. Greatly moved he remarked to General Sir Hastings Ismay, 'Never in the field of human conflict was so much owed by so many to so few.' These words were rather irreverently followed by . . . 'and for so little' when the men of the RAF heard these immortal words incorporated into a speech delivered at the House of Commons on August 20:

'The gratitude of everyone in our Island, in our Empire, and indeed throughout the world, except in the abodes of the guilty, goes out to the British airmen who, undaunted by odds, unwearied in their constant challenge and mortal danger, are turning the tide of world war by their prowess and devotion. Never in the field of human conflict was so much owed by so many to so few'.

Below: A Junkers Ju 88 making a low-level raid on a British airfield defended by a Bofors gun.

Below: A bombed Hurricane burns.

Airfield bombing

On August 16 Brize Norton was bombed: 46 aircraft were destroyed on the ground and 18 damaged. This was to be the pattern of the next phase in the Battle of Britain.

Saturday August 24 dawned fine and clear, and it was obvious that the attacks would restart. All the fighters in *Luftflotte* 3 had been moved to the Pas de Calais, the closest point to England. This meant they were not using up precious flying time over the sea. The attacks again centred on 11 Group because most of 10 and 12 Groups airfields were out of range for the German fighters. The enemy tried to mislead the radar by flying up the Thames estuary and then heading south. But by going the long way round they lost their fighter escort with their short-range tanks having only enough fuel for about 90 minutes total flying time.

No. 264 Squadron Defiants had now been added to the front line. The shortcomings of this aircraft were now well-known to both the RAF and Luftwaffe. Six were lost together with six crewmen on August 24; two aircraft collided while trying to scramble as Hornchurch was being bombed. By August 28 a further 10 had been lost together with seven crewmen. After this they were no longer used on daytime attacks.

Also on that fateful Saturday, 10 Group got warning of a large formation of enemy aircraft approaching. They were expecting Ju 87s, but when they scrambled they found they were Ju 88s which ferociously attacked Portsmouth town and docks.

German aircraft formations tended to split up over land. What radar stations reported as single formations would be reported later by the Observer Corps as several groups heading for different targets. This gave a confused picture on the plotting table and made it difficult to direct fighters to the enemy.

On August 30 the weather was again fine and looked likely to remain so for several days. The action was ever

Below: Heinkel He IIIs attack a British airfield. Spitfires can be seen on the ground in their blast pens.

increasing in intensity. That same day Do 17s entered the Thames estuary and attacked shipping. Meanwhile some 70 He 111s and Do 17s crossed the Channel with an escort of about 100 fighters. By noon all Park's available fighters were airborne. He therefore asked Leigh-Mallory to provide air cover to protect Kenley and Biggin Hill.

But Biggin was badly damaged by Ju 88s which came in at under 300 metres and dropped 16 450 kilogram bombs. One hangar was hit and there was a direct hit on a trench shelter. In all there were 39 killed and 26 injured. Most telephone lines were cut, along with gas, water and electricity mains. Kenley, Shoreham and Tangmere were also attacked. The electricity main was cut along 130 kilometres of coast, thus taking seven radar stations off the air. That left the only early warning of the enemy's approach over the south-east corner of England in the hands of the Observer Corps.

Manston, on the cliffs of the Isle of Thanet, was not only being bombed frequently but was being strafed by fighters coming in low over the sea. Morale was at rock bottom. Men who had taken shelter after the devastating attack of August 12 were still there, emerging only at night. It had ceased to function except as a refuelling airfield.

On August 31 radar stations were again attacked, although they were all working again that night. Biggin Hill was attacked twice more. Two of the three remaining hangars were hit. The next day Biggin was bombed three times. The third time a direct hit was scored on the ops room. WAAF telephone operators Corporal Elspeth Henderson and Sergeant Helen Turner were awarded the Military Medal for staying at their switchboard throughout the raid. That evening the ops rooms was set up in a commandeered butcher's shop in the village. The very next day Brooklands, where Vickers was building the Wellington and Hawker was building the Hurricane, was bombed.

The fact that the Luftwaffe had added aircraft factories to its target list gave sector airfields a chance to get patched up. In two weeks Fighter Command had lost 200 more Hurricanes and Spitfires than they had received, plus 231 pilots had been killed, wounded or were listed as missing. Sector airfields were badly damaged with Kenley and Tangmere barely surviving.

At the beginning of September, air supremacy was nearly in Göring's hands. For Dowding the only hope was to try and hold on for a few more weeks when Sea Lion would have to be shelved until 1941 because of the onset of autumn.

The mounting toll

There was now a shortage of almost everything, especially trained pilots. Fatigue was probably the pilot's worst enemy. It slowed down his reaction time drastically and sometimes fatally. Pilots were lucky to get a full night's sleep, let alone three nights in a row. There were cases of men landing their aircraft, relaxing for a moment, and actually falling asleep in the cockpit before the aircraft had taxied to a halt. Others turned to drink to unwind.

Apart from general fatigue there was stress. The enemy chose the time and the place for the battles. The RAF had to be constantly on the alert. Added to which there was the personal grief at the loss of friends, and the various physical injuries that could happen as a result of, for example, ditching an aircraft.

It was little consolation to know that, by September, there were few Luftwaffe pilots who had not been forced to ditch at least once. They too were suffering from exhaustion, but perhaps more from frustration at the constant changes in strategy. Dowding rotated the squadrons wherever possible. He brought pilots from the quiet of 13 Group to the hard-pressed south-east, thus freeing those from 11 Group to take a 'rest' guarding the northern industrial areas.

In July the training time had been six months long. By August 10 it was down to two weeks. A pilot might get his 'wings' after 90 hours but this did not make him operational. Another 200 or so hours were needed to reach this standard. But standards were lowered and new pilots began to get operational training in the

Right: An ambulance and fire tender rush to the assistance of a crashed RAF fighter pilot.

Below: A crashed Bf 109; parts of this aircraft may well fly again as part of a British aircraft.

squadrons themselves. The result was that the old hands couldn't be spared to teach the new men the modern techniques. The new pilots went into combat unversed. They were anxious to fight and disinterested in any words of caution.

Bravery is no substitute for experience. The loss of one experienced man was worth 10 Spitfires. The losses of the 'fresh pilot' squadrons was far greater than those of the supposedly tired ones. Between August 25 and September 2, 616 Squadron lost 12 aircraft and five men. Between August 28 and September 6, 603 Squadron lost 16 aircraft and 12 men. But tired 54 Squadron, between August 24 and September 3, lost just nine aircraft and one man, and 501 Squadron, between August 24 and September 6, lost nine aircraft and four men.

From August 24 to September 6, 295 fighters were destroyed and 171 badly damaged. Only 269 new and repaired Hurricanes and Spitfires were supplied to squadrons during the same period. During the whole of August 260 fighter pilots were turned out by Operational Training Units, yet casualties for that period were over 300. A full squadron was 26 pilots; the average in August was 16.

Park reported extensive damage to five of his forward airfields and to six of his seven sector stations. Runways were now carefully painted to merge in with the surrounding countryside. Decoy airfields were sighted some distance from the real thing. But still damage became too much for the airfield workers with their buckets and shovels. Outside help had to be

brought in using earth-moving equipment.

Another cause of irritation was the 'Big Wing' controversy between Park and Leigh-Mallory. Squadron Leader Douglas Bader and AVM Leigh-Mallory liked the idea of sending up a large number of defending aircraft together – the Big Wing. Park did not get early enough warning of the approach of enemy aircraft in time to scramble three squadrons and get them into formation at the right height and time. Even if he could it would leave too many targets, mainly his own bases, unprotected.

No. 10 Group had backed 11 Group whenever necessary or possible. But Park was angered that when he had asked 12 Group to protect his airfields, the protection had not materialized and both Biggin and Kenley were hit. With enemy aircraft returning home for lack of fuel the Big Wing theory was greatly enhanced. A great deal of bad feeling was caused which eventually cost Park his job.

Below: Fatigue was the pilot's greatest enemy.

Thanks to Lord Beaverbrook, Minister of Aircraft Production, aircraft were being turned out at over three times the rate of the Bf 109. British factory workers were working around the clock, seven days a week. In Germany however they were still working a six-hour day because Göring thought that it would harm morale to ask them to work longer hours. The bombing of aircraft factories was worrying. When the Vickers factory at Brooklands was bombed, 88 workers were killed and 600 injured. Work on the Wellington bomber was brought to a standstill for four days.

About 24 fighters were being written off each day. Some were being repaired by the Civilian Repair Organization (CRO). Churchill was only being told the write-off figures and so did not realize how bad the situation was. There were 288 fighters left. A mere 11 days supply.

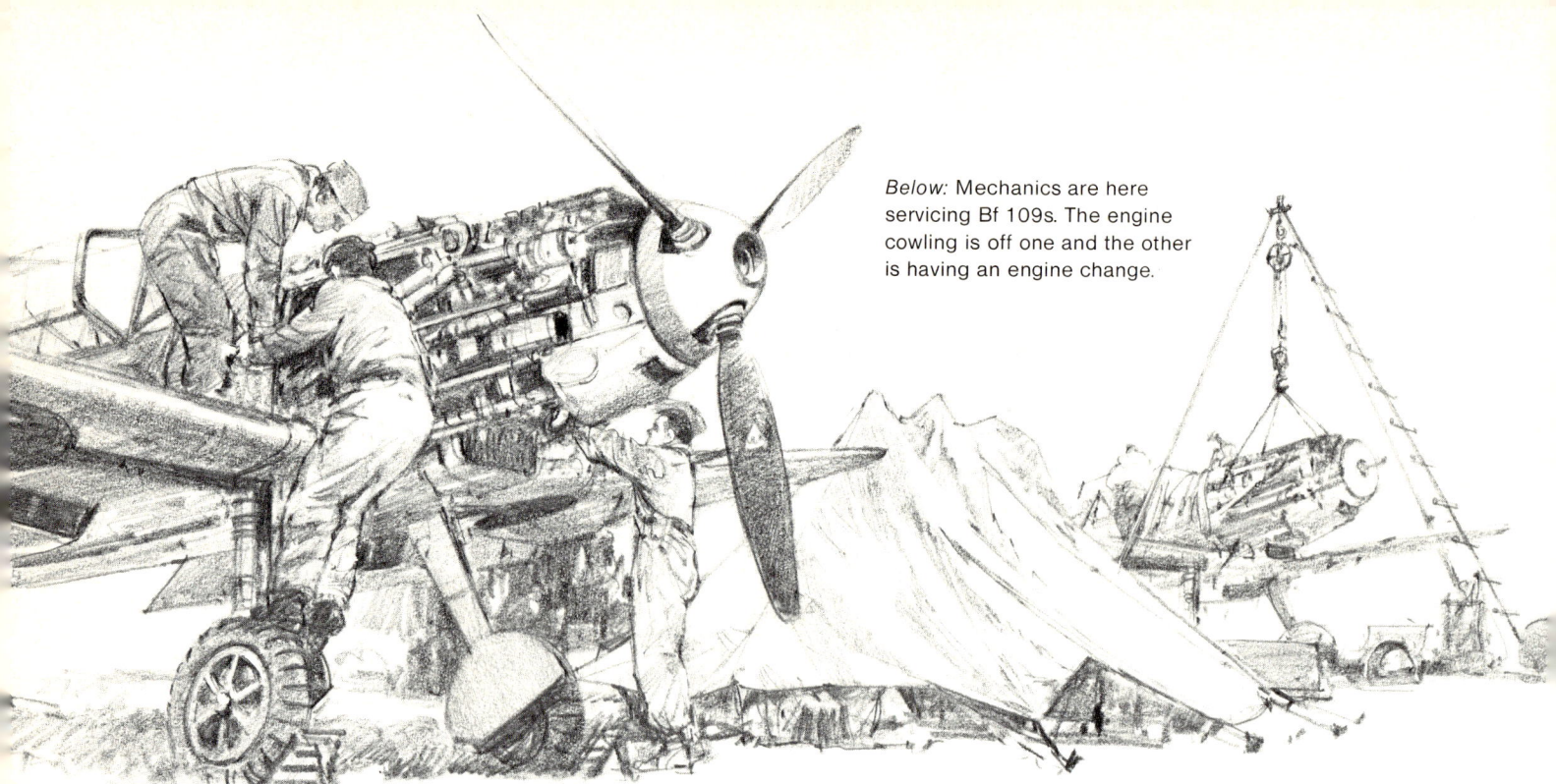

Below: Mechanics are here servicing Bf 109s. The engine cowling is off one and the other is having an engine change.

They also served

The Minister of Aircraft Production, Lord Beaverbrook, recognized the desperate need for fighters and geared his Ministry to their production, rather than the production of bombers, which the Air Ministry said were needed. Luckily most factories producing aircraft were in the Midlands, out of range of the Bf 109. But other factories took their share of harassment. Short Brothers at Rochester, Hawker's and Vickers' at Weybridge, Westland's at Yeovil and Supermarine at Southampton; all were attacked.

The Civilian Repair Organization (CRO) was started by Lord Nuffield and later came under the control of Beaverbrook. It salvaged every bit of a crashed plane, once the intelligence officers had inspected the German machines. Over half of the aircraft written off by squadrons because they could not be repaired on the airfield were repaired by the CRO. By mid-July they were repairing 160 aircraft a week, and eventually had a "while you wait" service, whereby aircraft which could be flown, albeit gently, would be repaired while the pilot waited.

The Air Transport Auxiliary (ATA) had been originally formed to carry mail, medical supplies, VIPs etc in aircraft piloted by personnel who, because of age or health, were not eligible for the services. In January 1940 women with flying experience were recruited to the ATA. Probably their most important job was to ferry trainers, fighters and bombers around the country.

Telephone engineers and electricians were in great demand. The radar stations and ops rooms relied heavily on telephones, teleprinters and electricity. Often the men would be repairing cables while the airfields were still under attack, or near an unexploded bomb.

After the raid there was always work for the bomb disposal experts. Delayed action bombs were particularly dangerous, and meant the evacuation of personnel. Rather than risk defusing them where they were, they would be towed away to a safe place and left to explode on their own. One such bomb took 49 hours to explode.

Groundcrew had to be quick. Aircraft caught on the ground were easy prey to bombers and fighters. There was the danger of attack and the men working on the machines were near petrol bowsers and ammunition boxes. Quick servicing of the aircraft was developed into a necessary art. Refuelling, re-arming, engine checking, oxygen replenishing and radio testing would go on simultaneously. Slit trench shelters by the dispersals meant that even when the airfield was about to be attacked, work could go on until the last moment. There were instances when a squadron of aircraft could return to battle within 10 minutes of having landed.

The Anti-Aircraft Command was a branch of the Army but was taken under the wing of Fighter Command. The Commander-in-Chief was Sir Frederick Pile, who was a friend of Dowding. The anti-aircraft guns were out-dated, and there was insufficient sighting equipment. It was realized that the search-lights could serve as a guide to enemy aircraft, and so they were only switched on to search for specific aircraft. There were also barrages of gas-filled balloons flown near key targets, which had the effect of forcing enemy aircraft to fly higher. The balloons, lights and guns could, and did, prove very discouraging to bombers anxiously searching for their target.

Nursing and ambulance staff performed many heroic tasks, and some died at their work. Firemen had some nasty jobs to do; not just those in the big cities with burning buildings and fractured water mains, but those manning fire engines on airfields who had to race to damaged aircraft making emergency landings, and try to get the pilot out before the whole thing exploded. Sometimes they were too late.

The various ground controllers, and those working in the operations rooms had the strange task of often plotting their own destiny. They knew well in advance that they were the target, and all they could do was move the relevant counters on the table, put on their tin helmets, and man the telephones until they went off the air.

Below: An example of team-work in difficult conditions. Spitfires return to their burning base to refuel and re-arm.

Weaponry

The Hurricane and Spitfire were each equipped with eight Browning machine guns. The idea of so many machine guns goes back to 1934, when it was reasoned that the speed of a modern fighter would be so much greater than that of a current bomber that repeated attacks would be impossible; the fighter would have to break off its attack or ram its prey. The two seconds during which the prey would be in the fighter's sights must be decisive. Experiments showed that eight guns firing 1,000 rounds a minute would be needed to get such a result. This requirement was built into the specifications which eventually resulted in the Hurricane and Spitfire.

After tests the American Colt machine gun was chosen. It was extensively modified and manufactured

Above: A Bf 109 at the firing butts. Its tail is jacked up to give the in-flight line of fire.

Below: An Oerlikon cannon used in German planes, and an armourer feeding the belt of bullets into the breeches in the wing roots.

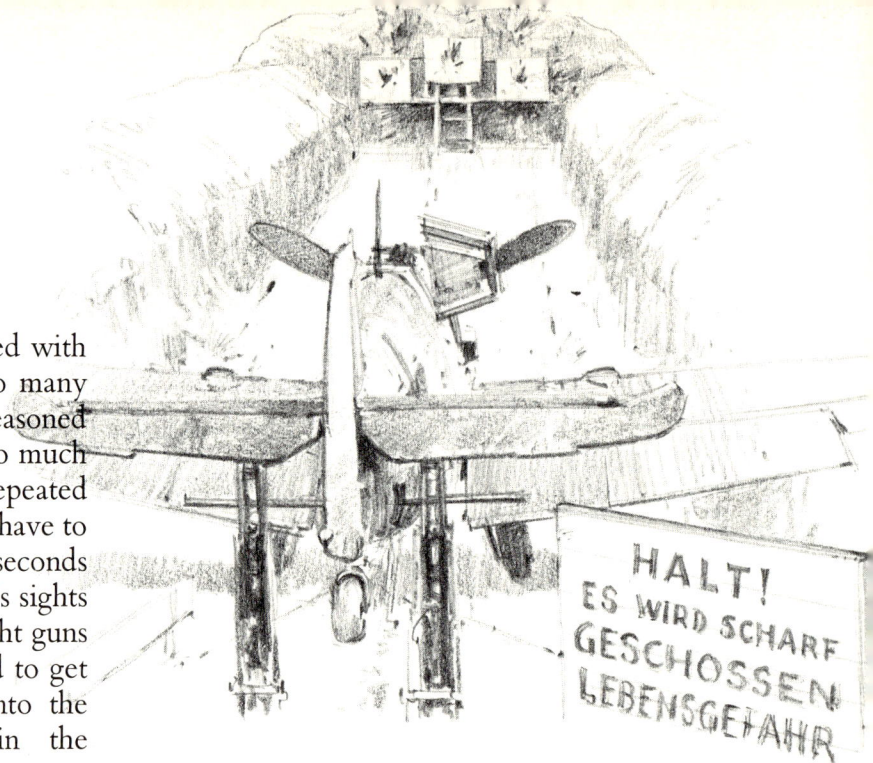

in Britain as the Browning. It was ideal, with a rate of fire of 1,200 rounds per minute. Thus the Blenheim, armed with five of these guns, could fire 100 rounds per second, while the Hurricane and the Spitfire could each fire 160 rounds per second. The Browning luckily proved reliable because, with the guns positioned in the wings, they could not be hammered to free them if they jammed.

The Hurricane was a very steady gun platform whereas the Spitfire, with its stressed wings, was a little less so. Ammunition was too scarce to be used in practice so pilots were opening fire before they were in range, and breaking away when they should have been opening fire. Despite RAF regulations which stipulated that the fire power from the Hurricane and Spitfire should converge 600 metres ahead of the aircraft, pilots got the armourers to change this to their own special preference (usually something like half the distance). It meant having to get closer to the target, but there was more likelihood of the target being destroyed.

There was trouble with guns freezing at high altitude. At first an oil and paraffin mixture was put on the guns, and this cured the problem of dry cold, but it was not a rust preventative. Flying through high cloud produced wet cold. The temporary answer to this was to stick fabric patches on the muzzles, which remained in position until the first round was fired. Later, heat from the engine was directed to the guns. The Germans could select their fire power. A thumb button on top of a control stick fired the wing guns, while a finger trigger fired those on the cowling. They also had an indicator to warn them when their ammunition was getting low. The RAF, having no such indicator, put tracer bullets at the end of the belt as a warning.

There were several types of bullet. Most popular was the De Wilde incendiary bullet. This had the added advantage of giving off a yellow flame on impact, and thus acting as an aim indicator. There were also armour piercing bullets, and the normal ball ammunition. These would usually be mixed in the guns as using the incendiary bullets exclusively would soon have ruined the barrels.

Below: The cockpit of a Spitfire with the pilot lining up a Bf 109 in his sights. When using the firing button there was a tendency to push the nose down at the same time.

More and more aircraft were being armoured, and so cannon were needed. The RAF experimented with 20-mm Oerlikon cannon on two Hurricanes and 30 Spitfires during the Battle, but they were unpopular with the pilots. Most of the enemy aircraft had cannon, which gave them a greater range than machine guns. The Germans, however, had modified their Swiss Oerlikon cannon to make it faster and lighter, but this resulted in a loss of velocity. With their Oerlikon the Luftwaffe was the first air force to use shell firing cannon as a standard fighter weapon. But it could hold only 60 rounds, which gave it only nine seconds of fire, while the RAF machines could fire for 14 seconds. Nevertheless, the aim was all important. Many aircraft limped home riddled with bullet holes because none had struck a vital spot.

Aces

The term "ace" had been used in the 1914-18 war for pilots who shot down five or more enemy planes. In the Second World War it was a loose term for a pilot who had several victories to his credit, or was an outstanding pilot. To become a so-called "ace" a pilot needed good eyesight, with the ability to spot aircraft in the distance. It was not easy spotting a camouflaged aircraft merging with the countryside beneath it, or searching for an enemy hidden in haze, or coming out of the sun.

Some Polish pilots would spend hours staring at flies on distant walls to strengthen their eye muscles. A pilot's reactions had to be good. He would have the enemy in his sights for only seconds or fractions of seconds. He must have a cool nerve. Some pilots had the fire from their Brownings converging a mere 230

metres in front of their aircraft. Thus, if they hit their target they would damage it badly, but they had to get very close. Once a man had destroyed an enemy aircraft his chances of survival improved because he gained in experience and confidence.

In the Luftwaffe 20 kills almost automatically won a Knight's Cross, and 40 kills added Oak Leaves to it. By the end of the war there were 35 Germans who had shot down 150 or more enemy aircraft. Erich Rudorffer ended the war as a top ace with 222 victories. The most successful fighter in combat against the Western Allies was Hans-Joachim Marseille who, when he died in an accident in 1942 aged 22, was credited with 158 victories. Heinz Bär joined the Luftwaffe in 1937. During the Battle he was credited with 17 victories, and by the end of the war, during which he had fought on every front and been awarded the Knight's Cross with Oak Leaves, Swords and Diamonds, he was credited with 220 victories. Werner Mölders, known as "Daddy" for his serious nature, was an ace in the Spanish Civil War with 14 victories, despite the fact he suffered from air sickness. By the end of 1940 he was credited with a further 55 victories. Adolf Galland is, perhaps, the best known German pilot of the period.

Left: Major Adolf Galland (with cigar) discusses tactical flying with Hauptmann Pingel.

He had such a liking for cigars that he installed a lighter and ashtray in his Bf 109. He received the Knight's Cross in August 1940 for 17 victories, and ended the war with 104 victories and Oak Leaves, Swords and Diamonds.

The British did not give medals when a certain number of enemy aircraft had been downed. They gave different medals according to the man's rank. For instance, Sergeant Frank Carey, who entered the RAF via Halton Apprentice School and was selected for pilot traning, was awarded the DFM (Distinguished Flying Medal) in January 1940. He later became an officer. Had he then been awarded the medal it would have been the DFC (Distinguished Flying Cross) awarded only to officers.

The men who are remembered as British aces are the men who caught the imagination of the public. Some of the top scorers are less well-known today than men who disposed of half the number of aircraft. Sergeant James H. "Ginger" Lacey, DFM, is one of the exceptions. He was the fourth highest Allied scorer during the Battle, and the top scoring Auxiliary. During the Battle he was credited with 15 victories including the He 111 which bombed Buckingham Palace on September 13. The top scoring British pilot was Pilot Officer Eric Stanley Lock, DSO, DFC, known as "Sawn Off" due to his lack of stature. He was credited with 16 victories, and by the time he died over France in August 1941 he was credited with at least 26 enemy aircraft. Flight Lieutenant Robert Stanford Tuck, DSO, DFC, who flew both Spitfires and Hurricanes, was credited with 10 kills, but is as well-remembered for his good looks, cigarettes smoked through a long holder and monogrammed handkerchiefs. Squadron Leader Douglas Bader is remembered less for his 'Big Wing' theory than for his "tin legs". He lost his legs in a flying accident in 1931 but fought back to operational flying. And there are a lot of men who died and who are remembered only by their families and historians.

The Allies

Some 3,080 men flew in the Battle of Britain and about 80 per cent were from the United Kingdom. Over 200 men came from the Commonwealth, and there were men from countries which had been over-run by the Germans: Czechoslovakia, Poland, Belgium and France. Some also chose to become involved, like the Americans, the Irish, and a single Palestinian. Churchill told General Ismay on July 12 that it was policy to encourage Allies to volunteer to fight with the British "to indulge their sentiments about the French flag and have them as representatives of a France which is continuing the war – the same to apply to Poles, Dutch, Czech, Belgian and Foreign Legion".

The top Allied scorer during the Battle of Britain was Sergeant Josef Frantisek. He had been a regular in the Czechoslovakian Air Force. He escaped to Poland and joined their air force, fighting with them for three weeks until he had to escape again, this time to Rumania. He reached the Middle East and there asked the French to send him to France, where he flew with the French Air Force until the fall in June 1940. He was awarded the *Croix de Guerre* before he escaped from the advancing Germans once again to join the RAF. He joined 303 Polish Squadron where he notched up 17 victories in one month before he was killed in a landing accident in October 1940. He was awarded the DFM, the Czech War Cross, and the Polish equivalent of the Victoria Cross: the *Virtuti Militari.*

In third place, behind Pilot Officer Lock, came Flying Officer B. J. G. Carbury, who was the top scoring New Zealand pilot, with 15 victories plus one shared. Flight Lieutenant Peterson Hughes, DFC, with a score of 14 plus three shared came in sixth place, followed by another New Zealander, Pilot Officer

Colin Gray, DSO, DFC, with 14 plus two kills. In ninth place came the top Pole, Flying Officer Witor Urbanowicz, DFC, with 14. The top scoring South African, Flying Officer C. R. Davis, DFC, had 11. The top scoring Canadian was Pilot Officer H. C. Upton, DFC, with a score of 10.

The Commonwealth pilots were mainly fliers who had come to Britain at their own expense before the war. As they were pre-war fliers they were among the first in battle, and they suffered heavy losses: 14 of the 22 Australians, and nine of the 22 South Africans died. Adolph Gysbert Malan was a South African. Known as "Sailor" because he joined a training ship at 13 and later became first mate with Union Castle, he volunteered for the RAF in 1935 and was a Flight Commander by the time he saw action in May 1940. By the end of July he had the DFC and bar, and later the DSO and bar. He was credited with 35 kills by the end of the war. Johnny Kent, a Canadian who learned to fly when he was 16, came to England in 1935 and joined the RAF on a Short Service Commission. He was with 303 Polish Squadron and was awarded the *Virtuti Militari,* as well as the DFC and bar, and was credited with 13 victories by the end of the war.

The Poles and Czechs had to master the rudiments of the English language, as well as the RAF flying procedure, and were usually given a rank below that which they had held at home. The Polish squadrons were commanded by RAF personnel, but "understudied" by Poles. No. 303 Squadron became operational by accident on August 30. They were on a training flight, saw enemy aircraft, attacked, and shot down a bomber. This squadron had such a high score that the Intelligence Officer was asked to quiz them particularly closely. When they corroborated each others stories, Group Captain Vincent decided to fly with them on their next sortie. He soon saw that their figures were facts. In three weeks 303 had the highest score in 11 Group: 44 in five days over London alone.

About a dozen Free French flew under Fighter Command during the Battle of Britain. The first of them did not become operational until September 11. These were given British markings and painted with yellow undersides so they should not be mistaken for enemy aircraft. Don Kingaby, then a Pilot Sergeant

Right: Some of the emblems of nations who provided allied pilots in the Battle of Britain.

with 92 Squadron, remembers the time in October that Xavier de Montbon, whose Spitfire had met a Bf 110 head-on, returned to base with cannon shell jammed through the windscreen. Second Lieutenant J. De Mozay, familiarly known as Moses, joined 1 Squadron in October 1940 and ended the war with the DSO, DFC and bar, and *Croix de Guerre.*

There were three Americans in 609 Squadron: a barnstormer, a professional parachutist, and a light plane flier. In October 1940 they helped to form the first American Eagle Squadron. During 1941 all three were killed over Britain.

Below: Flight-Lieutenant Johnny Kent of 303 Squadron (Polish) climbs into his Hurricane.

London bombed

Hitler had forbidden raids on London, but in early September there were two conflicting views. *Generalfeldmarschall* Hugo Sperrle, of *Luftflotte 3*, wanted to continue attacking Fighter Command airfields. *Generalfeldmarschall* Albert Kesselring, of *Luftflotte 2* pointed out that, if hit too badly, the fighters would be withdrawn from southern England to a position where bombers would have to go unescorted. If London were bombed the fighters would be forced to defend it, and could then be destroyed.

In fact, on the night of August 24-25, London had been bombed in error. Some 170 bombers had, apparently, intended to raid Rochester and the oil tanks at Thameshaven, but bombed the City of London and surrounding boroughs instead. Berlin had been bombed in retaliation. But after the bombing of Berlin, Hitler rescinded his instructions concerning London being a prohibited area. The switch in target was sudden. Fighter Command was still preparing for another onslaught on the sector airfields, and thus the raid on London was carried out virtually without hindrance.

This change of tactics proved a godsend for Fighter Command. They could now repair their airfields. As Churchill later said, by departing from the classical principles of war as well as from the hitherto accepted dictates of humanity, Göring made a foolish mistake.

At the outbreak of war 2,000,000 casualties had been forecasted. In fact the total civilian casualties caused by air attacks was 146,777 (60,595 killed and 86,182 seriously injured). Göring's aim was now to destroy Britain's capital and thus the Briton's will to wage war. Even had the former objective been successful, the latter did not necessarily follow (as shown later when German cities were subjected to heavy bombing. 'It isn't,' Lord Woolton said, 'the Government of this country that's going to war – it's the people'.

On Saturday September 7, Göring stood on the French cliffs to watch nearly 1,000 aircraft head for London. They were flying much higher than usual, at about 5-6,000 metres. The raid started at tea-time and went on until daybreak. The pattern of daylight attacks on airfields had now changed to one of night attacks on the City. The Surrey Docks were set ablaze and the flames acted as a beacon for further raids.

The Blitz had started, and was to continue for over 50 nights. Civilians did not panic. The Government had seen how refugees clogged the roads of Europe and prevented vital troop movements and had told the British people that the same thing must not happen here. Children had been evacuated from major cities months before. The people now got used to sleeping on the platforms of underground stations.

Two million Anderson shelters were distributed free to those earning less than £250 per annum. These were made of 14 sheets of corrugated iron and were buried in a one-metre pit in the garden. This was then covered with 45 centimetres of soil, and soon became a home to many. There were also public shelters, some of which could hold 1,000 people. Beds were moved under the stairs because this was considered to be the safest place in the house. Every employer of more than 30 people was required to supply a night fire watcher. Fires were left to blaze because water was in short supply. When the tide was out there was 15 metres of soft mud to cross before the hoses could be filled from the Thames.

Queen Elizabeth (now the Queen Mother) visited the East End of London in October and wrote to her mother-in-law, Queen Mary: 'I feel quite exhausted after seeing so much sadness, sorrow, heroism and magnificent spirit. The destruction is so awful and the people too wonderful – they *deserve* a better world'.

Night fighters

To find their way in the dark the German bombers used the *Knickebein* ('crooked leg') beam. It functioned like a blind landing system with dots to one side of the scanner beam and dashes to the other. A steady note told the pilot he was riding the beam. The British discovered *Knickebein* in June 1940, and gave it the code-name 'Headache'. They set up a jamming device, suitably code-named 'Aspirin', which transmitted dashes on the same frequency as the beam.

The Germans then switched to *X-Gerät*. He 111s equipped with special apparatus, and with specially-trained crews, flew along a beam that was intersected at various stages by three other beams. At the first inter-section the crew were alerted. At the second a time clock was punched. At the third, the time clock was punched again and the bombs released automatically.

It was far safer for bombers to operate at night, so fighters had to be adapted to deal with night flying. The Luftwaffe experimented with the Bf 109 as a night

Above: Night fighter pilots at dispersal wearing dimmer glasses to accustom their eyes to the dark.

Above: A Defiant gets an He 111 in its sights against a night sky lit up by searchlights and tracer bullets.

fighter and added searchlights to illuminate the enemy aircraft. But the fighters lacked the necessary endurance. In July 1940 a night fighter squadron was formed called *Nachtjagdgeschwader* I. These Bf 109s and 110s were to fly against Allied bombers over German territory, while the Ju 88s and Do 17s would try to catch the bombers near their home bases. The attacks near the home base were particularly demoralizing. An aircraft about to take-off or land lacks the speed or room to evade an enemy.

When London became the target there were only 92 guns to protect it. It was therefore thought best to leave the night sky to the night fighters of 11 Group. Night flying was in its early stages so few enemy aircraft were shot down. In 491 sorties in 46 nights, only 11 enemy aircraft were brought down. General Pile, the officer in command of Air Defence Artillery, withdrew guns from provincial towns and in two days had doubled the strength of London's artillery forces. On September 10 the barrage opened up under a blaze of searchlights. The RAF were told to keep away. The gunners were given a free hand to shoot at anything they heard. This had a good result on the morale of Londoners. They could now hear that something was being done in their defence.

Night fighters still patrolled the skies elsewhere. Prior to getting airborne the crew would wear dimmer glasses (like sunglasses) to accustom their eyes to the gloom. To see the enemy at night the fighter pilots had to fly low in order to try and silhouette the enemy against any available light in the sky.

The Beaufighter, a successful development of the Blenheim, was taken into service during July to September. It was equipped with wing-mounted machine guns and cannon on the fuselage, thus leaving the nose section free for radar. No. 604 AAF Squadron was one of those chosen to develop the use of airborne radar in night fighters. Flight Lieutenant John Cunningham, with Sergeant Jimmy Rawnsley as his radar operator, destroyed 20 German machines during the war. To conceal the fact that his Beaufighter was equipped with AI, it was said that Cunningham had been chosen for his exceptional night vision, which was increased by the large amount of carrots he consumed. British children were thus told to eat up all their carrots and be like the famous 'Cat's Eyes' Cunningham.

Battle of Britain Day

Sunday September 15 1940 is remembered as Battle of Britain Day. Hitler had postponed Operation Sea Lion until the 17th so nothing was now to be held back in reserve. For the Luftwaffe it was now or never.

On this day, Churchill and his wife were at 11 Group's underground HQ. At first all was quiet, but then news of approaching enemy aircraft came through. Their strengths were 40+, 20+, 60+; the numbers building up all the time. The counters were pushed across the map table following the paths of the aircraft. On the tote board lights flickered until there were only a few showing squadrons at readiness. All the others were airborne.

This was the time to put into practice all those lessons learned in the last few weeks. The RAF fighters would soon need refuelling and re-arming. If a fresh wave of enemy aircraft caught them on the ground they would be defenceless apart from the airfield's guns. So some had to be kept in readiness to take over the moment the first fighters were recalled. But the time did come when all the readiness lights were out. Park therefore asked Dowding for three squadrons from 12 Group to cover London and the airfields. They too were soon airborne.

Below: A damaged He 111 limps homeward to France, anxiously watched by a group of German soldiers.

Now there were no reserves, as a grim-faced Churchill learned. Then the counters took on a new pattern. The enemy were going home.

Had Churchill been above ground he would not have learned much about the battle raging overhead. A layer of cloud prevented Londoners from seeing dogfights in the sky at speeds of up to 400 kmph.

The first formation of enemy aircraft had arrived over London as Big Ben was chiming noon. They were met by the Duxford 'Big Wing' of 12 Group, made up of five squadrons commanded by Squadron Leader Douglas Bader. This was an impressive sight. The more so as the Luftwaffe had been assured that Fighter Command was down to its last 50 aircraft. The enemy aircraft broke formation and dogfights developed. The Luftwaffe fighter escort ran low on fuel. By 12.30 most of them were heading south. The bombers, deprived of their escort and with low cloud precluding precision bombing, jettisoned their bombs and headed for home.

The next attack started at about 2 pm. Pilot Officer Paddy Barthropp noted in his log that there were 'thousands of them'. Twenty-three squadrons were put up by 11 Group, five by 12 Group, and three by 10 Group. Despite the cloud Buckingham Palace was attacked and one bomb damaged the Queen's private apartments. But this incident, though it did little material damage, was a great propaganda weapon. It showed the people of the East End of London, where most of the bomb damage had occurred, that the Royal Family shared in their dangers. By 4 pm the raiders had returned home.

This was the climax of the daytime battles. The German losses (60) were the highest since August 18. By surviving this day Fighter Command forced Sea Lion to be postponed indefinitely. Hitler concentrated on another subject; Operation Barbarossa, the attack on Russia. Although Göring was still saying that the RAF could be destroyed in four or five more days, the morale of the Luftwaffe was very low.

Right: Spitfires and Bf 109s join in a spectacular dogfight.

Epilogue

The battlefield of the Battle of Britain was larger than that of any previous conflict to be given that title. It covered much of England, but especially heavily hit was the south-east corner from Hampshire to Kent and north beyond London. It was also a three-dimensional battle, being fought up to 10 kilometres high in the sky.

It is called the Battle of England on the Continent, although it was the future of Britain which rested on the outcome of this battle; surely the longest battle in history. Wars have been fought and won in less time.

Historians differ in opinion on the start and end dates. The Air Ministry say the battle started on July 10 when Bf 109s and Stukas crossed the Channel in force. Others say that *Adlertag* (August 15) should be chosen. Some Germans even say that there was no battle as such. As a result, when some say that the battle was a

month longer than others, there is going to be a big discrepancy when statistics are quoted.

In the heat of battle, pilots could not be expected to verify victories. Several pilots may genuinely lay claim to an enemy aircraft at which they had all fired, thus adding one or two more to the score. This was particularly likely to happen when the 'Big Wing' was in action and three or more squadrons were all firing at the same group of aircraft.

It is interesting to note that the greatest number of aircraft lost in one day by one air force was not during the Battle. On May 10, when the Luftwaffe was opposed simultaneously by the forces of Holland, Belgium, France and Britain, and the Norwegian Campaign had not yet finished, they lost 304 aircraft destroyed and 51 damaged. The Polish campaign of September 1939 had cost them 285 aircraft lost and 279 seriously damaged. But even official figures can be mis-

Above: A crashed Dornier Do 17 in a Kent field is guarded by soldiers awaiting the arrival of an Intelligence Officer to inspect the wreck.

leading, as Churchill discovered when he found he had been given the figures for aircraft written off, which took no account of the aircraft which had been so badly damaged that they would be out of action for days.

The threat of invasion had been a very real one. Although, with hindsight, it would appear that the German plans for Operation Sea Lion were not very well thought out. All summer there had been rumours. Tired and jittery soldiers keeping watch on the Kent coast were constantly reporting sightings to their officers. During August the bodies of German soldiers were washed ashore on the south coast between the Isle of Wight and Cornwall. It would appear that they had been practising embarkation on invasion barges when the RAF Bomber Command attacked them. The discovery of the corpses led to rumours that the invasion had been attempted and repulsed. The rumour was allowed to spread. It was good for morale.

Reconnaisance photographs of the French Channel ports showed a drop in the number of invasion barges between September 18 and September 30 of from 1,000 to 691. British troops deployed to defend the country against Sea Lion were stood down for the winter. But it was not until June 1941, when Germany attacked Russia, that Britain felt safe from invasion.

The night bombing of London and the other cities did not bring about wholesale panic, as had been expected, with the population begging the Government to surrender before they were all killed. It had the reverse effect. It strengthened the resolve of the British people never to give in. It also proved a great leveler. When slum dwelling and Palace alike were bombed it struck at the very roots of the class system, which was not at all a bad thing. The bombing did not affect the war effort; factories and commerce continued their work and there was no great drop in production, as had also been expected. The most obvious effect was that the bombing gave Fighter Command a little less work.

There were mistakes in the way the Battle was fought by the British, and with hindsight such mistakes can always be found. But, basically, it was the organization and co-operation of Fighter Command which won the battle over the Luftwaffe. It was not a battle to be won or lost. It was a battle to survive. Without total air supremacy the Germans could not launch Sea Lion. Britain's survival shaped the outcome of the war, for the United States were impressed by what she had done. It was not that she was the 'Old Country' for many Americans; Germany was also the 'Old Country' for millions of others. But they had been hovering on the brink of what they had looked upon previously as a European war.

There was no sudden stop to the raids on towns and attacks on airfields. The air raid warning sirens would moan away for many months yet. At the end of September the Luftwaffe could, and did, muster 200 aircraft to attack Britain. In October so many German bombers raided Britain that it led to the longest and most widespread alert of the war. The most intensive bombing of London was yet to come. And still Flight Lieutenant Kingcombe remembers it as "all pretty routine really, after all, we were flying over our own country, and that helps – a lot".

Glossary

AAF: Auxiliary Air Force.

AI (Airborne Interception): The name for airborne radar.

AOC-in-C: Air Officer Commander-in-Chief.

ATA (Air Transport Auxiliary): Their most important job was ferrying aircraft around the country.

AVM: Air Vice-Marshal.

Ace: A fighter pilot officially credited with shooting down five or more enemy aircraft.

Ack-ack: Anti-aircraft, but more usually meaning anti-aircraft guns. It was taken from the term for AA used by radio operators.

Adler Angriff (Eagle Attack): Launched August 12, 1940.

Adler Tag (Eagle Day): Launched August 15, 1940.

Angels: Height per thousand feet. Thus 'Angels One-Five' meant 15,000 feet (5,000 metres).

BEF (British Expeditionary Force): An armed force sent to Europe at the outbreak of war to help defend France.

Bandits: Enemy aircraft.

Belly landing: A landing without the use of the undercarriage.

Big Wing: A large formation of aircraft. It was also known as the Duxford Wing after its home base, or Balbo, after the Italian ace who also favoured aircraft flying in large formations.

Blip: A spot of light on a radar screen that indicated the position of an aircraft.

Blitzkreig (usually abbreviated to Blitz): A swift, intensive method of warfare. It is commonly used to describe the bombing of London.

Bogey: Slang term for an unidentified aircraft.

CH: Chain Home radar.

CHL: Chain Home Low radar.

CRO: The Civilian Repair Organization which repaired damaged aircraft.

Cantilever: A type of wing structure in which no external bracing is used.

Circle of death: A defensive manoeuvre used particularly by Messerschmitt Bf 110s whereby they formed into a horizontal circle formation so that each could guard his neighbour's tail.

DFC: Distinguished Flying Cross.

DFM: Distinguished Flying Medal.

DSO: Distinguished Service Order.

De-brief: An intelligence officer would interrogate pilots about missions flown in order to pick up any useful scraps of information.

Ditch: To crash land, especially into the sea.

Flak (*Fliegerabwehrkanonen*): Shell burst fired from anti-aircraft guns.

Fliegerdivision or **Fliegerkorps:** The next link down the Luftwaffe chain of command from a *Luftflotte*. It could contain any number of aircraft from about 200 to 750, depending on the importance of the area in which it was sighted.

Float boats: The RAF version of the German safety island.

Free-fall: The drop before the parachute opens.

Geschwader: A Luftwaffe group usually consisting of 90 aircraft in three *Gruppen* (wings).

Gruppe: A Luftwaffe wing usually consisting of 27 aircraft in three *Staffeln* (squadrons).

IFF (Identification Friend or Foe): A method of identifying the friendliness or otherwise of an aircraft that is merely a blip on a radar screen.

In the drink: In the water.

Jagdgeschwader: Luftwaffe group fighter.

Jerry: Slang term for a German.

Kanalkampf (Channel Battle): The battle that took place in order to try and clear the English Channel so that the Germans could mount Operation Sea Lion.

Kapok: Silky down covering the seeds of the kapok tree. It was used for stuffing pillows and life jackets.

Luftflotte (air fleet): The link above the *Fliegerdivision* in the Luftwaffe chain of command.

Luftwaffenhelferinen (German WAAFs): Women serving in an auxiliary capacity in the Luftwaffe.

Maginot Line: A defensive wall of forts linked by underground galleries that protected the eastern frontier of France. It was named after the French minister of war.

Mayday: A distress call; an anglicization of *m'aidez:* help me.

Nachtjagdgeschwader: Night fighter group.

OKL (*Oberkommando der Luftwaffe*): Luftwaffe High Command.

OKW (*Oberkommando der Wehrmacht*): Combined High Command.

OTU: Operational Training Unit.

Operation Dynamo: The evacuation of the British Expeditionary Force from Dunkirk.

Pancake: To land.

Putsch: A revolt or uprising.

RAF: Royal Air Force.

RAFVR: Royal Air Force Volunteer Reserve.

RDF: Radio Direction Finding; an early form of radar.

RFC: Royal Flying Corps; the fore-runner of the RAF.

Radar: Abbreviation for Radio Detection and Ranging.

Rate of climb: The time taken for an aircraft to reach a specific height. To reach 6,500 metres, a Hurricane Mk. 1 took 16 minutes and a Spitfire Mk. 1 took 13 minutes.

Safety island: Rafts moored along the French coast as havens for downed Luftwaffe pilots.

Sea Lion: Code-name for the invasion of England.

Seenotflugkommando: Air-sea rescue unit of the Luftwaffe.

Scramble: Take-off.

Silk: A parachute.

Staffel: A squadron of nine Luftwaffe aircraft.

Stuka: An abbreviation of *Sturzkampfflugzeug*. Although generally meaning a 'dive bomber', Stuka came to mean the Ju 87 only.

Tail-end Charlie, or Weaver: The pilot at the back of the formation whose job it was to weave to and fro and guard the tails of the other aircraft. It proved an unsuccessful technique because he tended to run out of fuel before the others.

Tally-Ho!: An English hunting cry meaning that the prey is sighted.

Tote-board: The board at Fighter Command HQ on which was shown the availability of all the RAF squadrons.

Vector: With radar to tell them the position of the enemy, ground control could vector (direct) the pilot to the patch of sky where he would intercept the enemy.

Vic: V-formation.

WAAF: Women's Auxiliary Air Force.

The main events

1935
March 8: The existence of the illegal Luftwaffe was made public.

1939
Sept. 1: Germany invaded Poland.

Sept. 3: The British Prime Minister, Neville Chamberlain, made a broadcast in which he said no reply has been received from Germany to the British ultimatum "and consequently this country is at war with Germany."

Oct. 16: The first enemy aircraft to be shot down over Britain was an He 111 brought down by a Spitfire of 603 Squadron over the Firth of Forth.

Oct. 28: The first enemy aircraft to land on British soil was an He 111 forced down by Spitfires of 602 and 603 Squadrons.

Oct. 30: The first enemy aircraft destroyed on the Western Front was a Do 17 shot down over Toul by Pilot Officer P.W. Mould of 1 Squadron.

1940
April 9: Germany invaded Denmark and Norway.

May 10: German paratroops landed in Holland at dawn. Luxembourg was overrun. The Germans crossed the Belgian frontier.

May 10: Fokker D.XXXIs of the Royal Netherlands Air Force intercepted 55 Ju 52/3s and claimed 37 aircraft.

May 10: The German air force suffered the biggest loss of aircraft ever sustained in one day by one air force. Opposed by Holland, Belgium, France, Britain and Norway, they lost 304 aircraft destroyed and 51 damaged.

May 10: Chamberlain resigned as Prime Minister and was succeeded by Winston Churchill, who was previously the First Lord of the Admiralty.

May 14: Rotterdam is subjected to three hours non-stop bombing and Holland capitulated.

May 16: The withdrawal of the British Expeditionary Force from Europe was authorized.

May 17: After heavy bombing, Brussels capitulated.

May 26: Evacuation of the BEF —code-named Operation Dynamo — started from Dunkirk.

May 28: King Leopold ordered a cease-fire and Belgium surrendered.

May 10–June 16: The Battle of France, with Hurricanes of 1, 32, 73, 79, 85, 87, 501 and 615 Squadrons and Spitfires of 54 Squadron involved.

June 1: Göring ordered an all-out attack on the BEF at Dunkirk, and the Luftwaffe broke through the shield of British fighters covering the evacuation.

June 3: Operation Dynamo ended. Paris was bombed.

June 10: The Norwegian campaign ended. Italy declared war on Britain and France.

June 11: British bombers made their first attack on Italy when Whitleys of 10, 51, 58, 77 and 102 Squadrons raided Genoa and Turin.

June 14: The Germans entered Paris.

June 16: The French Premiership was taken over by Marshal Pétain, who asked the Germans for an armistice.

June 30: The Germans land on Guernsey.

July 4: The first Victoria Cross of the Battle of Britain was won by Acting Seaman Jack Mantle, who was on the HMS *Foyle Bank* in Portsmouth Harbour during a raid. The ship was the only one there with an anti-aircraft gun. Mantle manned it despite his leg being severed and suffering from other terrible wounds from which he died.

July 10: *Kanalkampf* began.

July 16: Hitler issued his Directive 16 ". . . I have decided to prepare . . . a landing operation . . ."

July: Aircraftman Bob Hollowday pulled a pilot from a blazing bomber. On return from hospital he entered another burning aircraft three times to rescue three crewmen amidst exploding ammunition. Surviving near-fatal burns, he was awarded the George Cross.

Aug. 12: *Adler Angriff* (Eagle Attack) was launched at British coastal radar and forward airfields.

Aug. 12–13: Flight Lieutenant R.A.B. Learoyd won the first VC for Bomber Command for his raid on an aqueduct of the Dortmund-Ems Canal in a Hampden.

Aug. 16 ("Black Thursday"): German attacks on Britain resulted in heavy losses for the Luftwaffe. Flight Lieutenant Eric James Brindley Nicholson won the only VC ever to be awarded to a member of Fighter Command.

Aug. 18: The first decisive defeat of the Stuka; 22 were lost or damaged, 17 from one *Stukageschwader* alone.

Aug. 20: In Parliament Churchill made his famous speech of indebtedness to "The Few".

Aug. 24: The start of relentless attacks on RAF airfields.

Aug. 24–25: London was bombed, apparently in error.

Aug. 25–26: Berlin was bombed for the first time by Hampdens of 61 and 144 Squadrons, Wellingtons of 99 and 149 Squadrons and Whitleys of 51 and 78 Squadrons.

Sept. 7: The Blitz started.

Sept. 13: Buckingham Palace was bombed. Bomber Command destroyed 80 barges intended for use in the invasion of Britain.

Sept. 15 ("Battle of Britain Day"): The climax of the Battle. Buckingham Palace bombed again. There were two main battles, at noon and in the afternoon, the latter being the larger. Over 300 RAF fighters were airborne.

Oct. 15: Heavy night attacks on London killed over 400 people, started 900 fires, cut train services and the underground railway system, and damaged docks, gas works, power stations and a reservoir.

Nov. 11: The first and only attack in strength by the Italian air force. Hurricanes of 46, 249 and 257 Squadrons claim seven Fiat BR 20 bombers and four Fiat CR 42 fighters, without loss to themselves.

Index

The main RAF and Luftwaffe units in the Battle of Britain

Ireland

England

• Farne Is

• Ponteland
HQ 13 Group

• Driffield
HQ Bomber Command

• Watnall
HQ 12 Group

• Brize Norton

HQ Fighter Command

• Stanmore

Uxbridge •
HQ 11 Group
■ London

• Box
HQ 10 Group

• Plymouth

• Biggin Hill

• Portsmouth

R • Foreness
R • Dover

Pevensey •
R • Rye

Ventnor •
• Poling
R

R

ATLANTIC OCEAN

ENGLISH CHANNEL

• Dunkirk
• Calais
• Wissant
(Stuka base)
Fl II

EG
• L

• Cherbourg

• Channel Is

• Le Havre
Fl VII
B

• Abbeville
B

• Dieppe

• Amiens •
B

• Brest

• Dinard
(Stuka base)

■ **Paris**
HQ Lf 3

• Vannes

• Le Mans
B

France